AMERICAN MURDERER

THE PARASITE THAT HAUNTED THE SOUTH

GAIL JARROW

WINNER OF THE YALSA AWARD FOR EXCELLENCE IN NONFICTION FOR YOUNG ADULTS

MEDICAL FIASCOES SERIES

AMERICAN MURDERER

THE PARASITE THAT HAUNTED THE SOUTH

GAIL JARROW

WINNER OF THE YALSA AWARD FOR EXCELLENCE IN NONFICTION FOR YOUNG ADULTS

CALKINS CREEK

AN IMPRINT OF ASTRA BOOKS FOR YOUNG READERS

NEW YORK

For information about permission to reproduce selections from this book,
please contact permissions@astrapublishinghouse.com.

Calkins Creek
An imprint of Astra Books for Young Readers, a division of Astra Publishing House
astrapublishinghouse.com

ISBN: 978-1-68437-815-9 (hc)
ISBN: 978-1-63592-829-7 (eBook)
Printed in China

Library of Congress Cataloging-in-Publication Data

Names: Jarrow, Gail, author. | Jarrow, Gail. Medical fiascoes series.
Title: American murderer : the parasite that haunted the South / by Gail Jarrow, YALSA winner.
Description: First edition. | New York : Calkins Creek, an imprint of Astra Books for Young Readers,
[2022] | Series: Medical fiascoes series | Includes bibliographical references and index. | Audience: Ages 10-17 |
Audience: Grades 5-12 | Summary: "Imagine microscopic worms living in the soil. They enter your body
through your bare feet, travel to your intestines, and stay there for years sucking your blood like vampires.
You feel exhausted. You get sick easily. It sounds like a nightmare, but that's what happened in the American
South during the 1800s and early 1900s. Doctors never guessed that hookworms were making patients ill,
but zoologist Charles Stiles knew better. Working with one of the first public health organizations, he and his
colleagues treated the sick and showed southerners how to protect themselves by wearing shoes and using
outhouses so that the worms didn't spread. Although hookworm was eventually controlled in the United States,
the parasite remains a serious health problem throughout the world. The topic of this STEM book
remains relevant and will fascinate young readers interested in medicine, science, history, and gross stories about
bloodsucking creatures"—Provided by publisher.
Identifiers: LCCN 2022004007 (print) | LCCN 2022004008 (ebook) | ISBN
9781684378159 (hardcover) | ISBN 9781635928297 (eBook)
Subjects: LCSH: Stiles, Charles Wardell, 1867-1941—Juvenile literature. | Hookworm disease—Southern
States—Prevention—History—19th century—Juvenile literature. | Hookworm disease—Southern States—
Prevention—History—20th century—Juvenile literature. | Public health—Southern States—History—
19th century—Juvenile literature. | Public health—Southern States—History—20th century—Juvenile
literature. | Necator americanus--Southern States—Juvenile literature. | LCGFT: Instructional and educational
works. | Illustrated works. | Biographies.
Classification: LCC RA644.H65 J377 2022 (print) | LCC RA644.H65 (ebook) |
DDC 616.9/654—dc23/eng/20220209
LC record available at https://lccn.loc.gov/2022004007
LC ebook record available at https://lccn.loc.gov/2022004008

First edition
10 9 8 7 6 5 4 3 2 1

Designed by Red Herring Design
The text is set in Garamond and Trade Gothic.
The titles are set in Tungsten and Bison.

TABLE OF CONTENTS

FOR CAROLYN, WHO MADE ME A BETTER WRITER

This Kentucky farmer was only thirty-five years old, but he looked much older. Too sick to work, he depended on charity to survive. Eleven members of his family were killed by the same creature that infected his body—the American Murderer.

CHAPTER ONE

VAMPIRE

"The disease . . . is primarily a 'poor man's' malady."

—Charles Stiles, American scientist

EARLY ONE MORNING IN NOVEMBER 1908, A TRAIN SLOWED down to pick up passengers at a southern railroad station. Peering through his railcar's window, a traveler from Iowa pointed to a deathly pale, hunched-over figure standing on the station platform.

"What on earth is that?" he asked his two companions, wondering what could make a young man look so emaciated and broken down.

His friend, who had grown up in the South, explained that the man was probably one of the local tenant farmers.

The Iowan was shocked. He was used to the robust look of midwestern farmers. "If he represents Southern farm labor the South is in poor luck," he said.

The third traveler, a scientist, had seen many similar people. In fact, he had been studying them for several years, and he knew exactly what was wrong with the man on the platform. He informed his friends that they were looking at a victim of America's bloodsucking murderer.

This vampire thrived in the warm southern climate. It lurked on the ground outside rural homes, schools, and churches. Invisible to its potential victims, it waited until one of them passed by. Undetected, it hitched a ride, burrowed in through the skin, and tricked the person's body into allowing it to stay. The intruder hid deep in the host's gut for years, anchored in place by sharp fang-like mouthparts.

Day by day, one drop at a time, the vampire devoured blood from its unsuspecting victim. At first the person suffered few ill effects. But when more invaders followed —and they usually did—his or her body became home to hundreds, sometimes thousands, of the tiny creatures.

Before long, the daily blood loss was enough to weaken and sicken the host. The person was transformed into a dull-witted, frail individual with a blank stare and shuffling gait—just like the man on the platform.

The scientist had learned many of the American Murderer's secrets. He understood how it attacked the human body. He was aware of the damage it did. And he was convinced the vampire could be stopped—must be stopped!—from slowly sucking the life and energy out of millions of men, women, and children. He was determined to end this medical fiasco—one that most of America didn't know existed.

CHAPTER TWO
WORM SCIENTIST

"The little worm . . . has acquired a bad reputation lately."

—E. Bugnion, Swiss physician

CHARLES WARDELL STILES'S FATHER AND GRANDFATHER expected him to become a minister. They both had devoted their careers to preaching from Methodist pulpits, and it seemed natural to them that he would do the same. Charles had his own ideas. He was fascinated by animals, not religion.

Charles was born on May 15, 1867, in Spring Valley, New York, a small town north of New York City. He spent his boyhood exploring the nearby woods and fields, where he gathered specimens for his bedroom nature museum. Charles had collections of bugs, butterflies, and other creatures—both dead and alive. Curious about what was inside an animal's body, he dissected frogs and earthworms.

One day he found a dead cat in a vacant lot and decided to add its skeleton to his museum. First he removed the cat's fur, flesh, and organs. In order to detach the muscles from the bones, Charles realized he'd have to boil down the rest. Since no one was home to object to his plan, he filled one of his mother's large pots with water, put it on the stove, and dumped in the cat's remains. With the water on a slow boil, Charles went outside to play with a friend. He forgot about the pot on the stove until he smelled a stench and saw smoke coming from the kitchen.

Charles didn't get the new addition to his museum as he hoped. The water had boiled off, and the cat skeleton was burned into a foul mess.

DETOURS

Growing up in a minister's household, Charles had to follow certain rules. Sunday was reserved for religious activities. He was permitted to devote the hours after church services to singing hymns, walking and reflecting in the graveyard, or reading the Bible. Forced to choose, Charles opted for reading.

To make the task less boring, he turned it into a puzzle. Using the French he'd learned in school, he translated a French Bible into English as he read. Charles liked the challenge so much that he spent his Sunday afternoons translating German, Latin, Italian, and Greek Bibles. Although he didn't realize it at the time, this knowledge of languages would later prove useful.

Right before Charles entered high school, he moved with his parents and older sister to Hartford, Connecticut. He had good grades in his classes and excelled in languages, but Charles was more interested in playing baseball, football, and pranks than in studying.

On days off from school, he enjoyed helping out at a local surgeon's practice. Medicine appealed to Charles, and the surgeon suggested that he go directly to medical school after high school. This was a path that potential doctors could take in the nineteenth century.

Yet when the time came, Charles respected his father's wish that he attend Wesleyan University, a Methodist college in nearby Middletown, Connecticut, where his father once studied. Although Charles agreed to go, he had no intention of being a minister. He preferred science.

Charles's college career there only lasted until the middle of his second year. He developed severe headaches, which he blamed on eyestrain from reading with poor light, and he had to return home. Eyeglasses ended his headaches, but the unexpected weeks away from Wesleyan led Charles to a decision. If he was going to pursue biology, he wanted to do it somewhere else.

The world's best scientists taught at universities in Germany and France. Charles convinced his father that a European education would provide better training in biology and medicine than Wesleyan. With his family's support, nineteen-year-old Charles sailed for Europe later that winter.

His language skills helped him adjust to lectures at several colleges in France and Germany. Within a few months, Charles enrolled at the University of Berlin, where he studied for two years.

Charles Wardell Stiles (1867–1941), about age twenty-six, in Washington after receiving his German doctoral degree

After taking courses in zoology, botany, physics, chemistry, and anatomy, Charles decided he wanted to focus on animals, not humans. He was intrigued by worms that lived inside other animals, often causing harm to their host. The study of these parasites, called parasitology, was a new field of zoology. Determined to learn as much as possible, Charles left Berlin to train with the world's parasitology experts at Germany's University of Leipzig.

THE WORM WITH HOOKS

One of the worms he studied was named *Ancylostoma duodenale*, a member of a group known as hookworms. Hookworms gained their nickname because some types had hooklike structures on the tail end, which were part of the male's reproductive organs. Charles learned from his professor, a leading authority on parasitic worms, that *Ancylostoma duodenale* had only been discovered about fifty years earlier.

In 1838, Italian doctor Angelo Dubini (1813–1902) performed an autopsy on a peasant woman in Milan as part of his research into disease causes. He noticed a tiny white worm, about one-third of an inch long (8 mm), attached by its mouth to the mucous wall of her small intestine. When he examined the worm under a microscope, Dubini realized that it was unlike any of the human intestinal worms previously described by scientists.

Four years later, during another autopsy, Dubini spotted the same kind of worm again. This time he used a more powerful microscope so that he could sketch the worm in detail. Inside its mouth were four toothlike structures that Dubini described as curved hooks.

Now alert to this new worm, he found it in other dead bodies, sometimes in great numbers. Eventually, he saw it in 20 of the 100 human cadavers he dissected in his further study of the worm. This creature wasn't rare, but it was easy to miss. A doctor had to cut open the intestine and inspect the mucous lining carefully.

Dubini was aware that other parasitic worms could cause illness, usually because they were stealing nourishment from the host and using it for themselves. Yet the infected people he dissected had died from a variety of ailments. The only common symptom was weakness and emaciation, conditions that many hospital patients exhibit before they die.

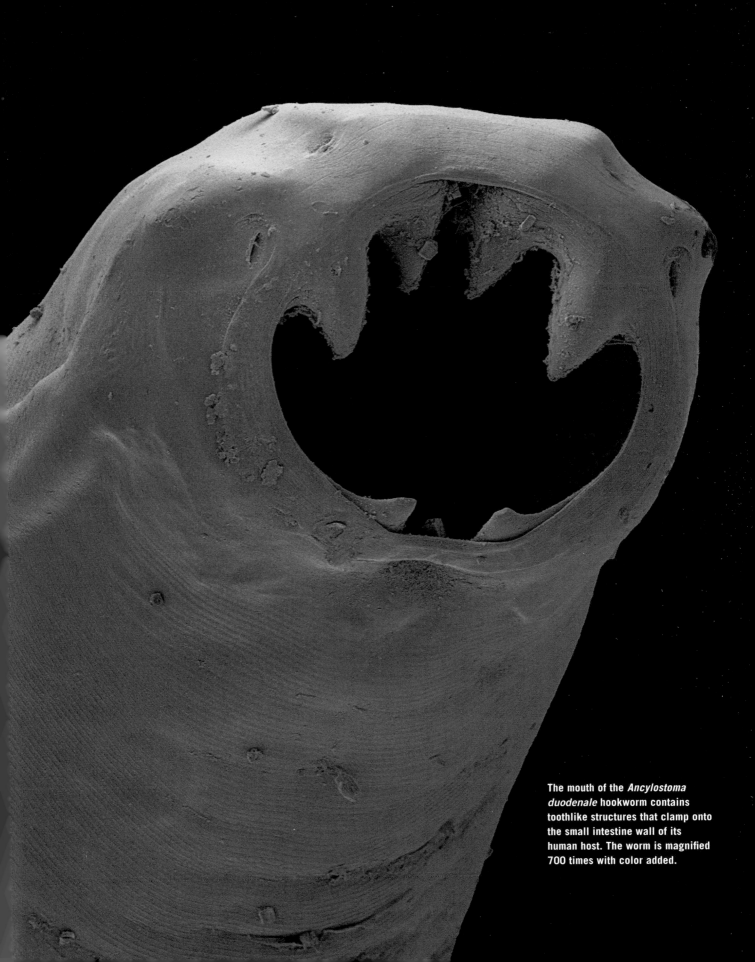

The mouth of the *Ancylostoma duodenale* hookworm contains toothlike structures that clamp onto the small intestine wall of its human host. The worm is magnified 700 times with color added.

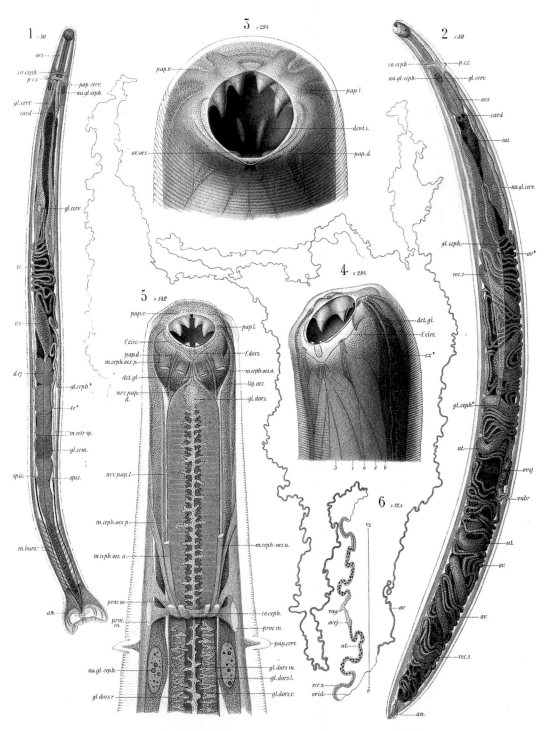

Illustrations of the internal organs of a male (on the left) and female *Ancylostoma duodenale*. The hooklike structures on the male's tail are part of the reproductive organs. The three drawings in the center show details of the hookworm's head and teeth. The worms range from about 0.3 to 0.5 inches long (8 to 13 mm) with males being slightly smaller than females. Drawings by A. Looss, 1905

In 1843, Dubini published a detailed description of the worm, its features, and its differences from similar parasitic worms found in humans and other animals. He gave it the name *Ancylostoma* (Greek for "hooked mouth") and *duodenale* (referring to the duodenum section of the small intestine where he saw most of the worms).

THE EGYPTIAN DISEASE

After Dubini's discovery, doctors in Egypt and Brazil also reported seeing *Ancylostoma* in the intestines of autopsied bodies. But no one had evidence to connect the worm to a specific disease.

A clue came from a German doctor, Wilhelm Griesinger (1817–1868). While practicing medicine in Cairo, Egypt, Griesinger frequently saw cases of severe anemia, called Egyptian chlorosis. This disease had been known in Egypt throughout its long history. Patients were so fatigued that they couldn't work, and their skin was unnaturally pale or yellow. Based on his experience, Griesinger estimated that at least a quarter of Egypt's population suffered from some degree of this illness.

In 1852, he performed an autopsy on a twenty-year-old man with chlorosis who reportedly died from diarrhea. When the doctor cut open the young man's small intestine, he found it filled with fresh blood. Thousands of *Ancylostoma* hung from the mucous lining like leeches.

Griesinger concluded that the man had bled to death. In an 1854 medical journal, he proposed that chlorosis was caused by the parasites in the man's intestine. Later, other doctors confirmed Griesinger's hypothesis by finding hookworms inside the bodies of dead anemia patients.

Diseases similar to chlorosis, known by different names, were described in writings from ancient times. Besides severe anemia, symptoms included pica—the strange habit of eating dirt or other nonfood material such as wood, charcoal, or chalk. For at least two hundred years, doctors had reported these symptoms in people living in tropical climates throughout the world, including Africa, India, Caribbean Sea islands, and parts of South America. It appeared that *Ancylostoma* could be the cause. But many questions remained.

Unlike most intestinal worms that pass from the body in feces, only the eggs of *Ancylostoma* leave the body—thousands of them at a time. One researcher tried to infect himself by swallowing large amounts of these eggs. After two months, he still had no disease symptoms and found no eggs in his feces. That meant adult worms were not living in his body.

Scientists were able to observe hookworm eggs hatching into minute larvae in a warm, moist environment outside the human body. Yet none of the larvae developed into the adult stage that doctors had seen in the small intestine of cadavers. How did the parasite get inside the body, take up residence, grow to adulthood, and produce eggs?

It was a mystery.

In this 1882 illustration, miners ride into the Gotthard Railway Tunnel for a day's work. The tunnel took ten years to construct as miners bored through the rocks. When it was finished in 1882, it was the longest tunnel on Earth, extending more than 9 miles (15 km).

THE SICK MINERS

Early in 1880, hundreds of workers fell ill while building the Gotthard Railway Tunnel under the Swiss Alps. The sick miners were so weak that they had to leave the tunnel site and go home.

For many, home was in northwestern Italy. Doctors assumed the men had miner's anemia, an illness previously seen in coal miners. This disease was thought to be caused by poor nutrition, dirty living conditions, and the lack of fresh air deep underground.

But the men did not recover after returning home. Instead they became worse. Over the next weeks, several died in a Turin hospital. Italian doctors performed autopsies. Clinging to the lining of each man's small intestine were tiny white worms. One doctor found more than 1,500 in a single person. He viewed them under a microscope and recognized the worms as *Ancylostoma duodenale*, the same parasite that caused Egyptian chlorosis.

By June 1880, more than 100 miners had died. As the year went on, physicians in Switzerland and Germany also reported severely anemic workmen from the Gotthard Tunnel. The doctors gave the sick miners a medication derived from ferns that was known to kill intestinal worms. It worked. The dead hookworms released their hold on the intestine wall, and the host's body expelled them in feces. Doctors identified the worms as *Ancylostoma*.

Medical experts knew that this worm appeared to cause severe anemia in tropical, lowland places such as Egypt. But the Gotthard Tunnel was located in the Alps, a cold and mountainous climate. How could the miners be infected with it?

The best explanation was that some of the miners came from warm, humid areas of Italy where doctors had observed *Ancylostoma*. The men likely brought the parasite to the tunnel within their bodies.

Miners routinely defecated on the ground inside the tunnel, and the waste was never cleaned up. The feces mixed with water that accumulated on the tunnel floor. Because the underground tunnel was wet and warm, the hookworm eggs and larvae survived. Miners often stood for hours in this water as they worked. Somehow—no one was sure how—the hookworms entered their bodies.

A recent photograph of an abandoned passage inside the old Gotthard Railway Tunnel shows the conditions under which miners worked from 1872 to 1882. The men were infected by hookworm larvae that survived on the moist ground of the tunnel.

The Gotthard Tunnel cases generated new interest in hookworms among European scientists. An Italian doctor discovered a more effective treatment than fern to kill and remove the parasites from the body—thymol, an oil derived from the herb thyme. Other researchers checked anemic workers in mines throughout Europe with conditions like those at the Gotthard Tunnel. When these miners were treated with thymol, they expelled hookworms and were cured of their anemia.

———————

Charles Stiles learned all about this research while studying parasites in Germany. But when the twenty-four-year-old finished his education and went home, most American doctors had never heard of *Ancylostoma duodenale*. The few who had read about the human hookworm were certain it hadn't come to the United States.

They were wrong. The parasite was already here.

CHAPTER THREE
UNLOCKING SECRETS

"Nature goes along its own hidden ways and does not tie itself to hypotheses and formulas."

—Arthur Looss, German scientist

CHARLES STILES HAD BEEN IN EUROPE FOR MORE THAN four years. He had trained with the most respected scientists in parasitology and earned his doctoral degree. In July 1891, he began a new job in Washington as a zoologist at the U.S. Department of Agriculture (USDA) in its Bureau of Animal Industry. Stiles had the expertise the Bureau needed to help farmers identify, treat, and avoid the parasites that sickened their animals.

THE MISSING WORM

The Bureau kept a collection of parasites that its scientists used in their research. Soon after arriving in Washington, Stiles looked through the specimens. He saw jars of hookworms that infected dogs, cats, cattle, and sheep. But there was no *Ancylostoma duodenale*.

Stiles reasoned that if domestic animal hookworms could survive in the United States, so could the human hookworm. *Ancylostoma duodenale* lived in Europe, Asia, and Africa. America was populated primarily by people who had come from those continents. Stiles guessed that the parasite probably infected people in the U.S., too, particularly where the climate was warm and humid.

Stiles (left) and zoologist Albert Hassall (1862–1942) working together in the USDA's Bureau of Animal Industry Division, around 1900. In 1892, the men organized the Bureau's parasite collection as a reference tool for researchers, veterinarians, and physicians. This collection continued to expand and is now part of the Smithsonian Institution's National Museum of Natural History.

Curious, he searched through American medical reports for signs of human hookworm disease—severe anemia, weight loss, pale or yellowish skin, and pica (dirt-eating). He discovered a few references to these symptoms in the southern United States going back to 1808. None of the reporting doctors connected the symptoms to a parasite, however. Stiles wasn't surprised. He knew that American doctors hadn't been trained in the past to diagnose hookworm disease.

In addition to Stiles's responsibilities at the USDA, he taught about human parasites at local medical schools. During one lecture at Johns Hopkins Medical School in nearby Baltimore, he brought up hookworm disease. "This malady must surely exist here more frequently than reported," he told the students.

In the audience was a respected professor, Dr. William Osler. Osler had written a popular medical textbook that included a description of hookworm disease. The book stated that no recent cases had been seen in the United States. Osler objected to Stiles's comment, which sounded to him like a criticism of American doctors. If it was actually present, Osler said, "a disease, as easily recognized as is hookworm disease, could not be generally overlooked."

Stiles thought it was a disease that *could* be overlooked when people weren't aware of its symptoms. The parasite was hidden from the patient and doctor, tucked away in the small intestine. Its eggs were only visible under a microscope—if a doctor knew to look for them.

Convinced that human hookworms infected some Americans, Stiles kept his eyes out for new cases mentioned in medical journals. During the next several years, he spotted occasional reports from southern doctors who had read about hookworm disease and believed *Ancylostoma duodenale* caused a patient's symptoms. They had found hookworm eggs in the feces.

Meanwhile, Stiles continued his mission of educating the American medical community about hookworm. In his lectures at Johns Hopkins, Georgetown University, and the U.S. Army Medical School, Stiles emphasized the same message. "If you find cases of anemia in man in the tropics or sub-tropics," he told medical students, "consider the possibility of hookworm disease." He explained that it was easy enough to confirm by using a microscope to check the patient's feces for hookworm eggs.

One student, destined to be an army doctor, didn't forget Stiles's message.

A CLUE IN PUERTO RICO

When the Spanish-American War broke out in 1898, Bailey Ashford, a young U.S. Army surgeon, traveled with the troops to Puerto Rico, a Spanish colony where some of the fighting took place. Ashford had attended the Georgetown University and Army Medical Schools, where he heard Charles Stiles lecture about parasites.

After the short war ended, the victorious United States occupied Puerto Rico. In August 1899, a devastating hurricane struck, and the U.S. Army set up a field hospital to treat sick Puerto Rican civilians. Ashford was assigned to care for patients there.

He noticed that many of them suffered from severe anemia. Weak and emaciated, they had grayish-white or pasty yellow skin. They seemed dazed, as if drugged, and were unable to answer even simple questions or carry on a conversation.

Local physicians told Ashford that these symptoms had long been common among the poor in Puerto Rico. The stricken usually never improved and eventually died in their weakened state. When the doctors checked a patient's stool, they didn't find the typical intestinal worms—tapeworm and roundworm—to explain the ailments. The Puerto Rican doctors attributed the illness to inadequate food, the climate, or malaria.

Ashford remembered how hookworm infections could cause anemia. He was aware that the adult hookworm

Bailey Ashford (1873–1934) spent his career in Puerto Rico dedicated to reducing the hookworm infections that led to thousands of deaths. After ten years, Ashford had overseen the treatment of 300,000 people, about a third of the island's population. He worked with local doctors to inform Puerto Ricans how to avoid reinfection by improving sanitation where they lived.

was rarely seen in feces, but the eggs were. Ashford examined the feces of a few patients. His hunch was correct. The hookworm eggs were there, "in great numbers."

After he treated a patient with thymol, dead hookworms passed from the man's body in his stool. Ashford gave the anemic man iron supplements to help him recover his strength. Soon the devastating symptoms disappeared.

When Ashford saw the success of his treatment, he repeated it with other patients. Using a microscope, he examined the adult hookworms they expelled.

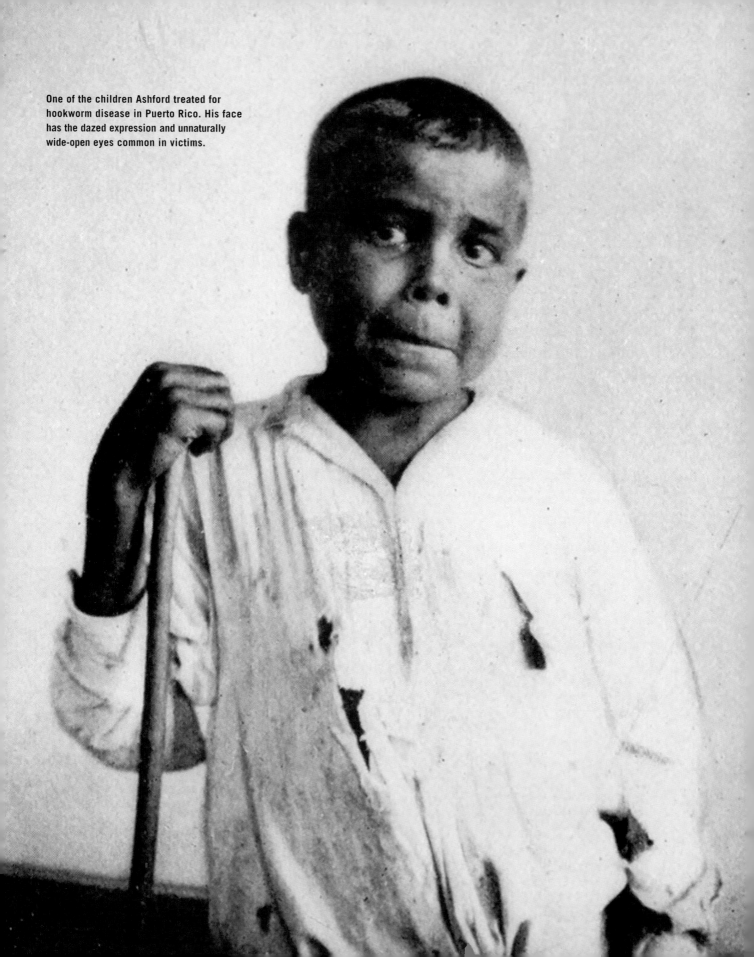

One of the children Ashford treated for hookworm disease in Puerto Rico. His face has the dazed expression and unnaturally wide-open eyes common in victims.

The worms looked like *Ancylostoma duodenale.* He had uncovered an epidemic of hookworm disease. Ashford later reported his findings in a scientific paper published in the spring of 1900.

Knowing he'd be visiting Washington, he saved a bottle of the worms to show Stiles. Ashford thought the parasite expert would be interested to hear that *Ancylostoma* was widespread in Puerto Rico.

At the time, however, Stiles was in Europe, not Washington. Before the Spanish-American War began, he had been sent by the USDA to assist the U.S. Embassy in Berlin, Germany. Traveling with him was his new wife, Virginia, whom he had married the previous June.

Germany charged that parasites in imported American pork had sickened its people. In response, the German government stopped the sale of U.S. meat. Stiles's job was to help resolve the situation. During his two years there, he was able to prove that the illnesses were originating from Germany's infected hogs and its own meatpacking plants, not from America. Faced with the evidence, the Germans lifted the pork embargo.

After Stiles returned to Washington from Germany with his wife and infant daughter, he resumed his duties at the USDA. But before he heard about Ashford's work in Puerto Rico, Stiles read of an exciting scientific breakthrough in Egypt.

Charles Stiles's wife, Virginia, and older daughter, Ruth, about 1903. They had a second daughter, Elizabeth, in 1905.

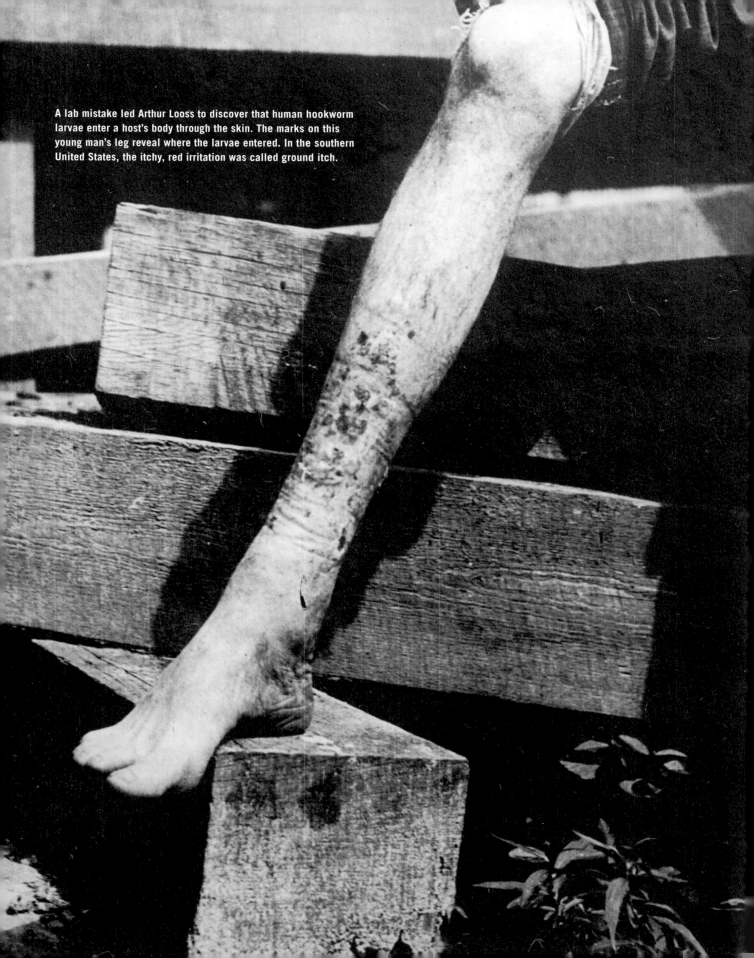

A lab mistake led Arthur Looss to discover that human hookworm larvae enter a host's body through the skin. The marks on this young man's leg reveal where the larvae entered. In the southern United States, the itchy, red irritation was called ground itch.

AN ACCIDENTAL DISCOVERY

While Stiles was tracking down pork parasites in Germany and Ashford was treating anemic Puerto Ricans, a German scientist made a startling discovery in Egypt.

Arthur Looss was interested in tropical medicine, including parasitic worms. He and Stiles had studied with the same parasite expert in Germany, and the two men were friends.

By the end of the 1890s, nobody had figured out how *Ancylostoma duodenale* entered the human body. Researchers demonstrated that swallowing hookworm eggs would not infect a person. Scientists didn't know when and where a larva transformed into the adult hookworm that spent its life feeding on the small intestine wall. Looss wanted answers to these mysteries.

Working in his Cairo lab in 1898, he mixed hookworm eggs into feces and soil. After a few days, Looss saw thousands of tiny *Ancylostoma* larvae on the soil surface, waving back and forth. He continued experiments with the larvae to learn more.

One day he clumsily spilled a drop of water filled with hookworm larvae on his hand. The water rolled off, but Looss's skin burned and turned red. He tried it again with another drop of water and larvae, and his skin reacted the same way.

This time Looss used a scalpel to gently scrape off the remaining moisture from his skin. Then he examined the water under the microscope. Most of the larvae were gone, but they left behind their empty worm skins. Looss realized the living larvae had entered his skin.

Where had they gone once they were inside his body? He began checking his feces for hookworm eggs. If he saw any, it would be proof that adult hookworms were living and mating in his small intestine.

After more than two months, he finally found eggs in his stool. During the period of his experiment, Looss occasionally felt tired. He believed this was further evidence that the hookworms were affecting his body. He treated himself with thymol, and dead adult parasites exited his intestine in his feces.

Looss had exposed a hookworm secret. He demonstrated that larvae penetrated his skin, traveled to his intestine, developed into adults, and produced eggs.

The scientist still had additional questions.

To investigate where the invading larvae traveled after entering the skin, Looss performed experiments on a human cadaver, an amputated leg, and volunteers. He also used dogs and the hookworms that attacked them. Eventually, he discovered more details about the human hookworm's life cycle.

After eggs leave a human's body in feces, they hatch and the larvae emerge. If the external surroundings are warm enough and moist (though not too wet), the larvae grow and develop. They crawl to the soil surface or to low vegetation and sway in the air, waiting to make contact with human skin.

Looss learned that a larva enters the host's skin at a pore, causing irritation and itchiness. It travels into the bloodstream and is carried to the lungs, where it leaves the blood vessels. The larva moves up through the lung's branches and the windpipe, and the host swallows it down into the digestive system. The larva settles in the small intestine.

Using its mouth, the larva attaches to the intestine wall, matures to adulthood, and mates with an opposite sex adult hookworm also living in the intestine. Females produce eggs which leave the host's body in feces. Looss calculated that the entire life cycle takes several weeks.

AN ALERT FROM TEXAS

Looss's discovery impressed Stiles. Now he understood how hookworm disease spread through the contact of skin with feces-contaminated soil. Many people in hot climates didn't wear shoes. They could be infected if their sanitation was poor and feces were scattered across the ground where they walked. The key to controlling hookworm infections was to prevent bare skin from meeting the larvae.

Once he was back in Washington in January 1900, Stiles resumed his study of hookworm cases in the United States. Ashford's Puerto Rico specimens confirmed that the parasite existed in the Americas. But Stiles noticed something puzzling. The specimens looked different from *Ancylostoma duodenale*. The worm's body was slightly shorter. Most striking were the cutting plates in its mouth instead of *Ancylostoma's* sharp, hooklike teeth.

More intriguing evidence surfaced. In Stiles's position at the USDA, he fielded parasite inquiries from doctors across the country. During the summer of 1901, a Washington doctor contacted him. He had heard Stiles talk about hookworm, and now the physician wondered about one of his Virginian patients in the hospital with intestinal problems. The doctor thought he might have hookworm disease.

Stiles visited the hospital ward with the doctor. Peering at the patients lying in the roomful of beds, Stiles immediately picked out the man even before the doctor pointed to him. The patient had all the external symptoms of a serious hookworm infection.

Stiles found hookworm eggs in a sample of the man's feces. After the doctor treated his patient with thymol, Stiles studied some of the dead adult worms expelled in the stool. The worms looked like the ones that Ashford brought from Puerto Rico.

Around the same time, a University of Texas medical school professor sent Stiles hookworms passed by several of his students. Stiles examined the worms under a microscope. They matched the ones from Ashford and the Virginia patient.

Charles Stiles was a parasite expert. He had read all the scientific research published about hookworms—animal and human. There could be no mistake. The specimens in his lab were not *Ancylostoma duodenale*. The human hookworm in North America was an entirely different species—one never described before.

In May 1902, Stiles published a scientific paper in which he announced that a second species of hookworm infected and sickened humans. "In the new world we have a special, heretofore undescribed parasite which caused uncinariasis [hookworm disease]." He wrote that this worm was causing extensive illness in the southern states, "although it is rarely recognized."

Stiles called it the New World hookworm, because the species had been found in the Americas rather than in Europe, Africa, and Asia (the Old World). He later gave this bloodsucking parasite a bloodcurdling name: *Necator americanus*, the Latin translation of American Murderer.

The head and part of the body of *Necator americanus*, the American Murderer, magnified 600 times and color enhanced. It shows the cutting plates in the mouth cavity. Adult females are about 0.4 inches long (10 mm) and as thick as a straight pin. Males are slightly smaller.

An early scientific drawing of the internal organs of a male *Necator americanus*, greatly enlarged from the actual size (tail on the left)

CHAPTER FOUR
THE LAZINESS GERM

"Hookworm children are apt to study
and learn with difficulty."
—Charles Stiles

STILES WAS CERTAIN THAT *NECATOR* INFECTED MANY
more Americans than anyone realized. But there was much to learn about
hookworm disease, and he was driven to investigate further.

His interest in parasites was shifting from worms that infected farm animals to
the ones that sickened humans. He was eager to have a new job that enabled him
to focus on medical parasites.

In the summer of 1902, the Public Health and Marine Hospital Service (PHS)
established the Zoology Division in its Hygienic Laboratory to study animal sources

of human disease, including parasites. That August, Stiles took his expertise from the USDA to the PHS, where he became head of the new division.

Stiles convinced his boss, Surgeon General Walter Wyman, that the PHS should find out how widespread hookworm disease was in the U.S. Because *Necator* hookworms needed a warm climate to survive, Stiles asked permission to visit a few southern states. He wanted to observe the residents and speak with local physicians. Wyman agreed, and in September, Stiles set off on his trip from Virginia to Florida.

U.S. Public Health Service

The Service was first established by the U.S. Congress in 1798 to care for sick seamen in marine hospitals. In the 1870s, the Marine Hospital Service began to focus on the control of epidemic illnesses such as yellow fever, smallpox, and cholera. It started the Hygienic Laboratory in 1887 to study diseases and their causes. The Laboratory was an early step in the federal government's funding of disease research, carried out today by the National Institutes of Health.

By 1902, when Charles Wardell Stiles took his position as head of the Zoology Division of the Hygienic Laboratory, the Service's new name was the Public Health and Marine Hospital Service. Ten years later, it became the Public Health Service, the name used today (and in this book). The PHS is now part of the Department of Health and Human Services and led by the U.S. surgeon general.

Charles Stiles in his PHS uniform. In 1902, he became head of the Zoology Division of the Hygienic Laboratory.

SOUTHERN SURVEY

Stiles knew from the Gotthard Tunnel cases and several outbreaks in European mines that hookworm disease sometimes occurred in miners. He visited the copper and coal mines of Virginia and North Carolina.

At many of them, defecation was forbidden inside the mine, and the workers usually used the surrounding woods. Stiles examined feces there with his microscope, and he found hookworm eggs. Next he picked out miners who looked anemic. When he checked their feces, he saw eggs in a few of the men. Still, the number of hookworm infections was far less than among European miners.

In Virginia, Stiles stopped at the state penitentiary and assessed about 1,200 prisoners. Those who had the physical signs of anemia were sent to the prison hospital and their feces checked for hookworm eggs. No one was infected.

After traveling hundreds of miles through Virginia and North Carolina, Stiles had seen limited signs of hookworm disease. Disheartened, he wondered if he was looking in the wrong places. He recalled reading that dog and sheep hookworm infections were more common in areas where the soil was loose and sandy. He decided to expand his search to counties with sandy ground.

Everyone in this Kentucky family is infected with a large number of hookworms. They exhibit one of the symptoms of hookworm disease—a bug-eyed stare. The younger children don't wear shoes.

In one South Carolina county, a local doctor took Stiles to the rural house of a person known to eat dirt, a symptom of hookworm infection. As soon as Stiles met the eleven people in the family, he recognized hookworm disease in them all. He checked the feces of one child and discovered hundreds of *Necator* eggs. He told the doctor that an inexpensive thymol treatment would cure the family.

While he and the doctor toured the county, Stiles spotted dozens of adults and children with the unmistakable appearance of a hookworm disease victim. The observations confirmed his suspicions. The parasite was infecting American southerners.

"I returned to my hotel in the most excited state of mind," he recalled, "and for three days I could hardly eat or sleep."

Most of the hookworm disease cases Stiles saw were among farmers living in sandy-soil areas. Some infected people told him that they hadn't been sick until they moved to the sandy region. If one person in the family was infected, the rest typically were, too. Stiles noticed that the worst cases were among children and women.

Afflicted people complained of diarrhea and a bloated abdomen. Their skin was paler than normal. Children were physically undeveloped. Adults didn't have enough endurance to perform even minor work, and they were usually poor because they couldn't earn a living. Some people had experienced these symptoms for years, and family members had died with the same ailments. None of them knew why they'd been plagued for generations. They just accepted it.

The rest of the community considered these people sluggish and lazy. Because pica was a common symptom, the infected were often mocked as "dirt-eaters." No one understood that the symptoms were not a sign of weak character or low mental ability. They were evidence of a tiny worm—actually hundreds of worms—slowly sucking blood from a victim's small intestine.

Stiles was disturbed to learn that most rural doctors didn't understand this, either, and they weren't treating their patients for hookworm disease. He discovered that these sickly people had been misdiagnosed as having the anemia caused by malaria, a disease carried by mosquitoes. In fact, tests showed that many of them had no malaria parasites in their blood. Instead, their feces were full of hookworm eggs.

This Florida man had a long-term hookworm infection. His arms and legs are thin, and his abdomen protrudes. Other common visible symptoms include pale skin, slumped shoulders, and a blank expression.

Southern Farmers

After the Civil War ended in 1865, the agriculture system in the South changed. The enslaved workers who had farmed the plantation land were now free. Large-scale landowners set up a new system to replace their enslaved labor by renting parts of their land to individual farmers, both White and Black.

A tenant farmer owned his own tools and mules, but he had to pay the landowner for use of the land. Frequently, the farmer needed an advance from the owner in the spring to buy seeds, fertilizer, and other supplies. He paid back the money after selling his crop at the end of the growing season.

A sharecropper farmer borrowed tools, mules, and supplies from the landowner. To pay for these and for his land rent, he gave the landowner a share of the crop he grew, often half.

These farmers tried to pay off their debt each fall. But most struggled to support their families, especially when the crop failed or selling prices tumbled.

Stiles learned that hookworm disease was common among poor farmers in some regions of the South. Farmers in Georgia hoe a field, around 1900 (top). A boy plows a Kentucky field in 1916 (bottom).

THE HOOKWORM REPORT

The majority of the medical community claimed that hookworm infections were rare in the U.S. Supposedly, the only people who harbored hookworms had recently come to America from another country with *Ancylostoma duodenale* already in their bodies.

But by the end of his tour, Stiles had no doubt that hookworms were widespread in the South and that the parasite was *Necator americanus*, not *Ancylostoma duodenale*. The farther south he traveled, the more hookworm disease he saw. He guessed this was because hookworm eggs and larvae couldn't survive freezing temperatures.

In some communities, he found that as many as half of the adults and 80 percent of the children had infections. Based on symptoms described in the medical literature and by southern doctors he met, Stiles concluded that *Necator* had been in the South for decades—maybe for more than two hundred years.

In late October 1902, the PHS printed a report of Stiles's tour in its weekly publication. He wrote that hookworm disease "is one of the most important and most common diseases of this part of the South, especially on farms and plantations in sandy districts."

Two young children with hookworm disease. They were likely infected through their bare feet. Hookworms were especially harmful to children, interfering with normal physical and mental development. In a 1903 bulletin to doctors, Stiles noted that a hookworm-infected boy or girl under age twenty often had the physical development of a child six years younger. Severely infected children had poor concentration and memory, which affected their learning and school performance.

Stiles stated that hookworm was more than a health problem. "The disease in question is resulting in loss in wages, loss in productiveness of the farms, loss in the school attendance of the children." People were wasting their money on drugs and doctors to find cures for their ill health. Nothing worked because they weren't being treated for the true cause—hookworm.

Stiles didn't mince words in describing the cause of the hookworm epidemic. Hardly any farm he'd visited had toilet facilities, inside or out. People defecated, he wrote, "at almost any place within a radius of 50 meters [about a half a football field] from the house." Hookworm eggs were everywhere.

"THE LAZY GERM"

Surgeon General Wyman recognized the importance of Stiles's findings. He wanted hookworm disease to get more attention than it had received in the Public Health Service publication.

In early December 1902, he asked Stiles to give a speech about his southern survey at the Pan-American Sanitary Conference in Washington. The audience included physicians and public health officials from countries in the Americas. Their goal was to improve health and prevent epidemics. Stiles was glad for the chance to warn about *Necator*.

In his talk, he explained how hookworm disease could be identified and cured. He described the way the bloodsucking parasite sapped energy and ambition from its victims. Although these people seemed lazy, they were infected by the American Murderer.

One audience member was a reporter listening for a subject to interest his newspaper's readers. When he heard Stiles describe a worm that made a person appear lazy, he knew he had his scoop.

He approached Stiles after the speech. Chuckling, the reporter asked whether "it might not be said that the 'germ of laziness' had been discovered."

Stiles replied, "Yes; you might call it that if you wish."

The next day, the reporter's story appeared on the front page of the *New York Sun* under the headline "Germ of Laziness Found?" The article poked fun at the idea that laziness, which was considered an undesirable trait by most Americans, could be the result of a disease.

When Stiles saw the newspaper, he was shocked. Hookworm disease was serious, and he was serious about it. He hadn't realized that the reporter would make hookworm infections seem silly.

Newspapers all over the United States and Europe picked up the story. One newspaper said of Stiles: "He has just returned from a sojourn among the laziest

The headline on the front page of the *New York Sun*, December 5, 1902

GERM OF LAZINESS FOUND?

40

DISEASE GERM MAKES CHILD VERY LAZY

DR. CHARLES W. STILES, OF WASHINGTON, DECLARES CHILDREN OF SOUTH ARE IMPERILLED BY GERMS.

HUNTING DOWN THE LAZY GERM.

Scientists Trying to Remove All Excuses for That Tired Feeling.

THE GERM THAT MAKES US TIRED

Newspapers made fun of Stiles's claim that laziness could be blamed on a disease. Headlines from Atlanta's *Semi-Weekly Journal* (left), the *Denver* [CO] *Republican* (top right), and New York's *The World* (bottom right)

people in the world, the 'crackers' of the south. . . . Dr. Styles [sic] is sure they are to be pitied rather than blamed."

Another teased, "The American scientist can rest assured that if laziness is a germ, work will cure it."

Several newspapers were sarcastic: "It is the privilege of the lazy man always to believe that he has the real thing and is not to blame for not liking work." And "There is only one danger. . . . The investigators are quite likely to be germ-bitten and become too lazy to carry their investigations to a finish."

But Stiles's report hit a nerve with a few southern newspapers. He had discussed a familiar group in the South—described by one North Carolina newspaper as individuals who were "weak in body and weak in brain power." Perhaps Stiles had explained why these people were stuck in poverty, generation after generation. If he could help them, one newspaper editor wrote, let him keep investigating.

Stiles was discouraged when the ridicule continued for months. Hookworm had been unscientifically labeled the Lazy Germ, and the suffering of its victims turned into a joke.

Yet as time went on, Stiles became thankful for the publicity. News of America's hookworm problem had reached more people. "It would have taken scientific authors years of hard work," he later wrote, "to direct as much attention to this subject."

Hookworm disease was finally out in the open.

All About Hookworms

"Plain Facts on a Dirty Subject"
—*Richmond* [VA] *Times-Dispatch*

By 1903, Stiles and fellow scientists had a good understanding of human hookworm and its life cycle. During the following decades, researchers expanded that knowledge. Today many—though not all—of hookworm's secrets have been revealed.

THE INVASION

Based on studies of ancient human remains and feces, researchers think hookworms have lived as human parasites for at least twelve thousand years. As people migrated around the planet, the hookworms went with them.

With slight differences, *Necator americanus* and *Ancylostoma duodenale* hookworms attack the body the same way. A hookworm egg exits the human host in feces. The egg hatches on the soil, and the first stage of larva emerges. Living off bacteria in the feces and soil, the larva develops through two more stages over several days. The eggs and larvae must stay warm and moist, and they cannot survive freezing temperatures. Shady conditions prevent them from drying out.

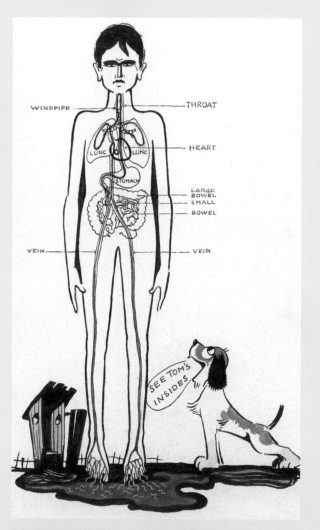

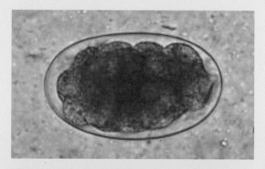

A hookworm egg as seen through a microscope. Doctors diagnose a hookworm infection by examining a sample of the patient's feces under a microscope and looking for these eggs. The more eggs, the more adults are living and mating inside the person's small intestine.

This drawing appeared in a 1920 booklet about hookworms distributed to schoolchildren. It shows the pathway of tiny larvae from the boy's feet to his small bowel (intestine).

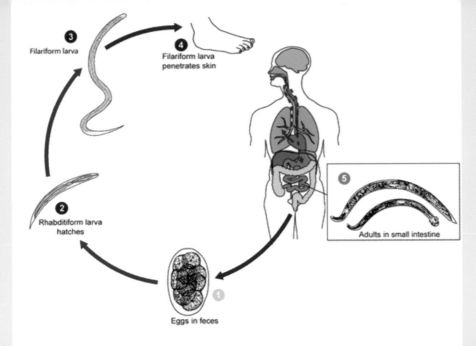

③
Filariform larva

④
Filariform larva
penetrates skin

⑤
Adults in small intestine

②
Rhabditiform larva
hatches

①
Eggs in feces

The diagram shows the life cycle of a hookworm from an egg to a larva to an adult inside the human host. Depending on the external conditions, the entire cycle can take three months or longer.

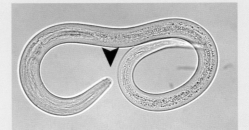

In the third stage, the threadlike larva is called a filariform. The filariform is more likely to thrive in sandy soil than in clay, because the loose sand allows it to move down below the ground surface out of the hot sun. The filariform larva doesn't eat. Instead, it goes in search of a human host by wiggling up from the soil surface to a slightly higher point, perhaps a blade of grass. To keep moist, the larva takes advantage of damp soil and morning dew.

Once in position, the larva waves in the air, an action called questing, as it waits for a host to pass by. Frequently, many larvae are grouped together close to the feces where they hatched. Larvae and eggs can be spread farther from this spot by a rain downpour or animals walking through the filth.

You won't notice a questing larva, because it is too small to see without a microscope. But if the larva makes contact with your exposed skin, such as a bare foot, it may enter your body.

With help from a chemical that it secretes, the hookworm larva penetrates your skin and enters your bloodstream. At the site where the larva burrows in, you may develop an itchy, red rash called ground or dew itch.

The filariform larva, shown here, lives in the soil where it waits to attach to the skin of a human host. Its mouth is at the center of the image (see arrow). This is the view through a microscope. The larvae are too small to see with the naked eye.

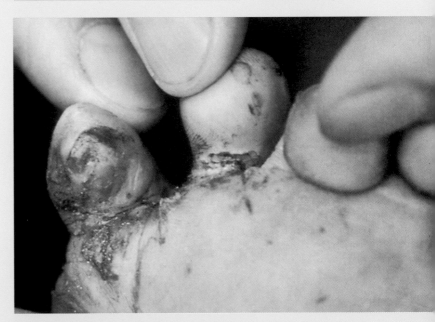

When the hookworm larva penetrates the skin, it causes an irritation called ground itch. The rash is itchy, red, and swollen. Several hookworm larvae entered this child's skin between the toes.

THE JOURNEY

The larva's journey through your body continues as your bloodstream carries it to the heart and from there to the lungs. In your lung, the larva again uses a chemical to break out of a capillary and into one of your lung's small air sacs. The larva makes its way through your lung's airway branches and up your windpipe. If many larvae have invaded, you might wheeze or be short of breath while they move through your lungs.

When you swallow, the larva is carried down the esophagus to the stomach and into the small intestine, where it will mature into an adult.

The adult latches onto the mucous lining of your small intestine. *Necator americanus* does this with cutting plates inside its suction-cup-shaped mouth. *Ancylostoma duodenale* has toothlike structures instead. Both kinds of hookworm bite into one of the tiny projections on the intestine wall, called villi, sucking blood and tissue for nourishment.

The hookworm keeps your blood flowing by releasing a chemical that prevents clotting. After devouring a piece of your intestine wall for a few days, the adult hookworm detaches and moves to a new area. It will take two or three days for your body to stop the bleeding and heal the original spot.

Ancylostoma larvae can enter the human body in an additional way that *Necator* can't—through the mouth. When fields are fertilized with human feces, *Ancylostoma* larvae contaminate the soil and may crawl onto crops. Children playing or farmers working in the soil get larvae on their hands. If a person puts dirty hands into his mouth or eats unwashed and uncooked vegetables, the larvae are swallowed to the small intestine where the hookworms settle, mature, and mate.

THE BLOOD SUCKING

People infected with just a few hookworms may not feel sick. But those with more may have abdominal pain and diarrhea, and they often lose their appetite. Some develop the urge to eat dirt or other nonfood substances (pica), which may be the body's reaction to a nutritional deficiency.

The most serious effect of a hookworm infection is caused by the parasite's bloodsucking. A person infected with 110 *Necator* adults loses about 1 teaspoon (5 ml) of blood a day. The *Ancylostoma* worms suck out at least five times as much. That's enough to cause serious health problems if it continues for a long period, if hundreds or thousands of worms infect the small intestine, or if the human host has a diet low in iron and protein.

The steady blood loss reduces the number of iron-enriched red blood cells in the human host. Without adequate amounts of these cells, the blood doesn't supply enough oxygen to the body's tissues and organs. The result is anemia. An anemic person is fatigued and lacks the strength and energy to perform physical work.

In this magnified view, an *Ancylostoma* hookworm attaches to the small intestine wall with its mouth (see arrow) and sucks up blood and tissue.

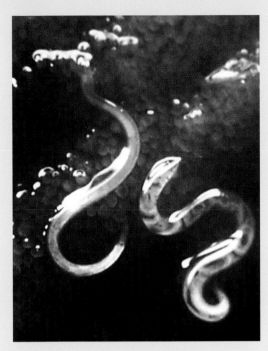

These adult dog hookworms are attached to the small intestine of their canine host. *Necator americanus* and *Ancylostoma duodenale* behave the same way inside a human host.

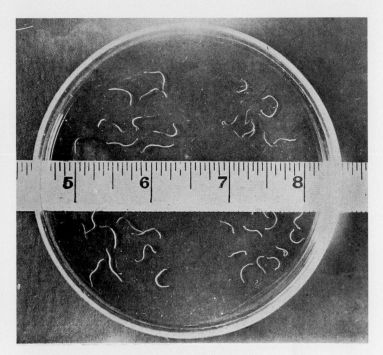

The photograph shows adult *Necator americanus* hookworms next to a ruler marked in inches.

Although hookworms alone usually don't kill a patient, the weakened body becomes more susceptible to other deadly ailments such as pneumonia, malaria, tuberculosis, and typhoid fever. Those illnesses were common in the early twentieth-century South.

A pregnant woman and her baby are at risk from a hookworm attack when the mother is heavily infected and already has low iron levels from an insufficient diet. Her baby may not survive because it is born too early or weighs too little. The mother may die from the stress on her body of pregnancy and birth.

Children are also harmed, especially if they don't eat enough nutritious food. The bloodsucking parasite reduces iron and protein in the body to dangerous levels. That slows physical and intellectual development. When a child is constantly reinfected, these effects may be irreversible even if the hookworms are eliminated.

MAKING MORE HOOKWORMS

A mature male and female hookworm mate in the small intestine, and the female lays eggs that pass from the host in feces. A *Necator* female lays from 5,000 to 10,000 eggs a day, while *Ancylostoma* lays two or three times as many. Because the eggs don't hatch until passed outside, hookworms can't multiply inside the host.

Scientists still don't completely understand how hookworms resist the human body's immune system. Somehow, probably by using chemical secretions, they evade the mechanisms that attack other foreign invaders such as bacteria and viruses. *Necator* lives in its host's small intestine for three to five years or more before dying; *Ancylostoma* usually a year or two.

Recent research indicates that a person's genetic makeup likely affects how susceptible or resistant he or she is to a hookworm infection.

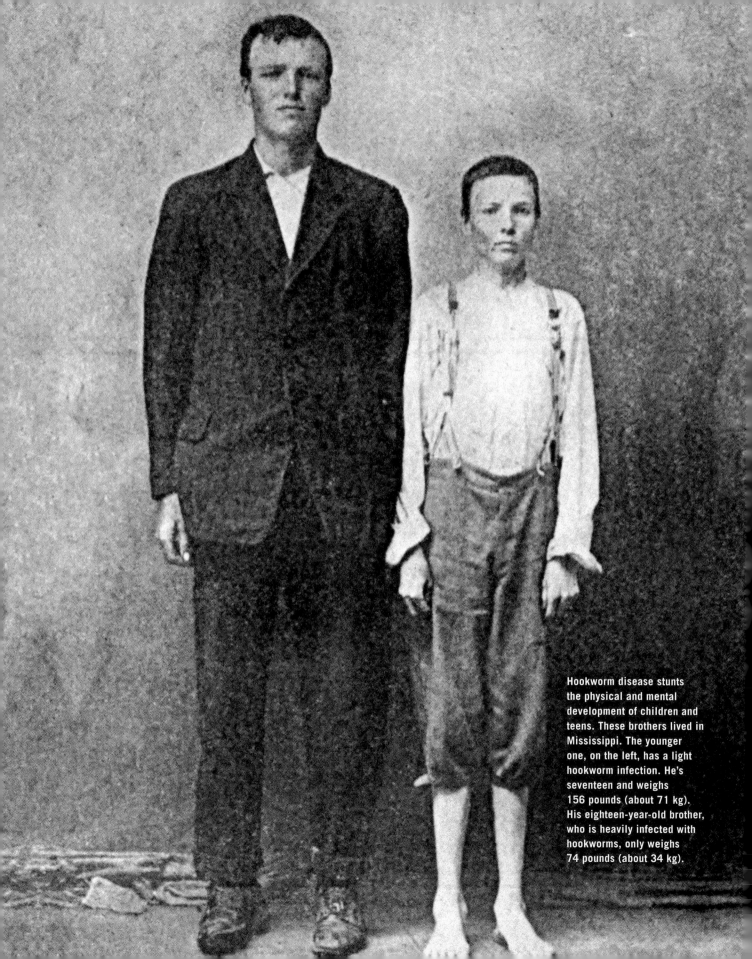

Hookworm disease stunts the physical and mental development of children and teens. These brothers lived in Mississippi. The younger one, on the left, has a light hookworm infection. He's seventeen and weighs 156 pounds (about 71 kg). His eighteen-year-old brother, who is heavily infected with hookworms, only weighs 74 pounds (about 34 kg).

CHAPTER FIVE

BATTLING NECATOR

"I believe that there are millions of people in our Southern States who are affected by the hookworm who can be saved."

—Charles Stiles

A S CHIEF OF THE HYGIENIC LABORATORY'S ZOOLOGY Division, Stiles was responsible for investigating diseases spread to humans by rabbits, ticks, and parasites such as roundworms and whipworms. But his primary interest remained hookworms.

Part of the PHS's mission was to educate doctors about health problems in their communities. So with Surgeon General Wyman's blessing, Stiles wrote informational bulletins about hookworms and conducted new research into *Necator*.

This young Mississippi woman suffered from a moderate case of hookworm infection. Her visible symptoms include sloping shoulders, a vacant expression, and bulging eyes. Her physical maturation had been slowed by the infection. She was abnormally short, and her breasts hadn't developed.

BACK ON THE ROAD

Whenever his PHS schedule allowed, Stiles traveled through the South to learn more about the parasite and spread the word about hookworm disease. He discovered that many doctors still didn't know how to recognize or treat a hookworm infection. Practically none of the public had heard of it.

During a trip to Florida, he stopped by a farm with a local doctor. All seven members of the family were emaciated and anemic-looking. When Stiles heard that fifteen children were buried in graves behind the house, he asked the doctor what had caused those early deaths.

"I do not know what the disease is, but if you can tell me what is killing *that girl there*," the doctor replied, pointing to a scrawny child whom he called a dirt-eater, "you will know what killed the other fifteen children."

One close look told Stiles what was wrong with her. Like the surviving members of her family, she had the symptoms of severe hookworm disease.

Stiles visited farms, cotton mills, hospitals, and orphanages. Over time, he examined 10,000 people and reported on his work in articles published by the PHS. He learned that many southerners were so used to feeling anemic and sick that they didn't consider their malady a medical issue. If they did seek help, their doctors treated their symptoms as the result of malaria, kidney problems, or digestive ailments. Yet Stiles believed the correct diagnosis was hookworm infection.

He thought *Necator americanus* was a key reason for "the inferior mental, physical, and financial condition of the poorer classes." The tiny parasite was holding these people back from success in life.

He knew the problem could be fixed.

A SIMPLE CURE

During his travels, Stiles spoke to state health departments, groups of doctors, and community members. He showed them hookworm eggs and *Necator* adults in photographs and through a microscope.

Stiles told people that, for about fifty cents, hookworms could be eliminated and hookworm disease cured. To convince audiences that the treatment was easy, he carried along a kit containing powdered thymol in capsules and Epsom salts. Stiles explained that the infected patient swallowed a dose of thymol. Two hours later, the patient took Epsom salts to help the body expel the dead worms. Within a day, the person was usually free of the parasite.

Stiles recommended that a doctor supervise the treatment because thymol was dangerous if not taken correctly. After treatment, the doctor should reexamine the patient's feces to confirm that the medicine had killed all the hookworms. If there were eggs present, adult worms still survived inside the small intestine. Then the patient received a second treatment. Some infected people required several before they were hookworm-free.

Stiles's presentations persuaded many southern doctors who had never heard about hookworm disease. When he described the symptoms, they realized that they'd observed the same signs in their patients. Now able to identify hookworm disease, these physicians could handle the problem.

Eventually, Stiles gathered strong allies among the southern medical community, and they educated others. A member of the Georgia Board of Health told his colleagues, "In no other serious disease does the victim suffer so long, in no other condition is he for such a period a menace to those about him, and in no other malady of such gravity is treatment so rapidly and surely successful."

In North Carolina, Stiles heard how this knowledge saved a life. A mother came to her doctor's office with her

Although hookworm eggs were invisible to the naked eye, people noticed other parasites such as tapeworms and roundworms in their feces. The infected were willing to pay for remedies, called vermifuges, to get rid of intestinal worms. This 1889 advertisement is for a tonic that claimed to do that . . . and more. Few of these medicines cured anything. In the early 1900s, the cure for hookworm was thymol, administered under a doctor's care.

pale and anemic baby. The doctor wasn't sure what was wrong until he saw large areas of ground itch all over the child's body. The mother hadn't been worried about the rash. She said it always happened after she placed the baby on the sand while she hung out the laundry nearby. The woman had no idea that her child was near death because hookworm larvae had invaded and caused a serious case of hookworm disease. Fortunately, the doctor recognized the symptoms and knew how to cure the baby.

Stiles had little patience with physicians who denied the existence of hookworm disease. He accused them of giving their patients worthless medicines instead of diagnosing and treating the real problem.

Some of those doctors reacted to his verbal attacks by pointing out that Stiles wasn't a physician, just a meddling Yankee outsider. They weren't impressed by his

Privies

In his articles published by the PHS, Stiles included drawings of badly built privies. This one (top left) shows human waste accumulated on a pile and leaking onto the surrounding soil. Farm animals spread feces (and hookworm eggs) on their feet throughout the yard. Rainstorms washed the waste into wells and streams, allowing the bacteria of intestinal diseases like typhoid fever and dysentery to infect those who drank the water. Flies carried bacteria-laden waste on their legs. In the caption of a similar drawing, Stiles wrote, "Is a privy of this kind near you, supplying your home with flies that smear human excrement over your food?"

At a minimum, Stiles recommended a sanitary privy with buckets to collect the waste (bottom left). He told people to toss dry dirt or powdered lime over the waste to neutralize odors and keep away the flies that spread bacteria to food. The buckets should be emptied regularly, ideally once a week, and the waste buried at least 2 feet (60 cm) underground away from a water supply. A door at the back swung down to block animals. Screened openings and an airduct provided ventilation while keeping out flies.

European training and parasite expertise, and they didn't accept that they might have missed an ailment that was so widespread.

Stiles didn't care what his critics said. People could be cured if their doctors were competent. And the victims' suffering could be prevented with a few changes in the way they lived.

BUILD AN OUTHOUSE!

Based on his knowledge of *Necator*'s life cycle, Stiles was certain that thymol treatments alone weren't going to solve the South's hookworm problem. Thymol didn't provide lasting protection against the parasite, and a person could be reinfected. Hookworm disease was so common, Stiles wrote, "not because the country air is particularly favorable to its development, but simply because so little attention is paid to the proper disposal of the fecal discharges."

The only way *Necator* eggs left a human body was through feces. Residents of towns and cities were more likely to have indoor toilets and a municipal sewer system. At the very least, their homes had an outhouse (privy). With people living close together, neighbors and local governments insisted on basic sanitation to prevent foul odors.

Stiles was appalled at the lack of any kind of sanitation on most southern farms. Families instead used the nearby yard, woods, or fields to urinate and defecate. At some farms Stiles visited, the entire area around the house reeked of excrement. Even when there was a crude privy, human waste accumulated on the ground surface, leaking from the open back.

That wasn't all. Stiles discovered that at least 80 percent of rural schools and churches lacked privies, too. At schools, students used the bushes. Boys went on one side of the building, and girls on the other. Frequently, they were barefoot, exposing them to hookworm larvae lurking on the contaminated ground.

After witnessing these conditions, Stiles was less surprised that so many rural southerners were infected, but that anyone was not.

In his conversations with farmers and his speeches to civic groups, Stiles frankly described the dangers of polluting the soil with feces. The human waste was spread around when animals walked through it or when farmers used it to fertilize gardens and fields. This soil pollution allowed hookworms to pass among people, constantly reinfecting them.

He explained to audiences that hookworms entered the body through skin. Because the parasites had to stay moist to survive, the risk was greatest when the ground was muddy or the grass wet. Wearing shoes would protect the feet.

But parents couldn't afford to buy shoes for children who quickly outgrew them. Besides, children were used to being barefoot, which they considered far more comfortable, especially in warm months. Their unprotected feet encountered hookworms at home, school, and church.

Stiles was blunt. He told rural southerners that the solution to the hookworm problem was well-built and carefully maintained sanitary privies. His audiences weren't used to someone talking about feces and privies, and many were offended by his indelicate language. He insulted people by saying that their family had worms because their homes were filthy and their children were shoeless.

After one of his presentations, the local sheriff assigned a bodyguard to Stiles throughout the rest of his stay in the area. The sheriff informed him that some members of the audience had been so outraged by his speech that Stiles wasn't safe.

CHECKING THE MILLS

As part of his 1902 southern trip, Stiles had visited several cotton mills to learn whether hookworm disease affected the employees. The mills employed large numbers of White workers, who lived in villages built by the mill owners. The mills rarely hired Black workers.

While walking through the mills, Stiles had carefully observed the workers, alert for signs of the condition called cotton-mill anemia, an ailment with the same symptoms as hookworm disease. He found that mill workers under age twenty were most affected and showed evidence of stunted growth.

Stiles's microscopic examination of a few workers' feces revealed hookworm eggs. Many of the anemic workers told him that they once lived on farms. Stiles

Cotton Mill Workers

By the 1880s, southern cotton mill owners were successfully competing with textile mills in the North. Because cotton was grown in nearby fields, the owners saved on shipping. They also had a cheap source of labor to turn the cotton into cloth.

Many White tenant farmers were eager to leave the hard farming life for the steady wages and easier work of a mill job. Some of them spent the warm months farming in rural areas and moved to jobs at the mills during the winter.

Entire families had jobs in the mills, including children as young as eight. They were on the job for ten or eleven hours a day for five days a week, plus five hours on Saturdays. Despite the low pay, with two parents and the children working, families earned more money than they had as farmers. Still, many of them lived in poverty.

Three children photographed at their home in a South Carolina mill village, 1908. Like most of their friends, they were barefoot much of the time. The older boy had already worked in the mill for four years.

Some of these young workers at an Alabama mill in 1914 didn't wear shoes even when on the job.

supposed that those who moved from rural areas had brought hookworms with them and that the parasite was responsible for cotton-mill anemia.

In 1907, the U.S. Department of Commerce and Labor asked Stiles and the PHS to do a more thorough investigation of anemia at the mills. The request was in response to charges by state and national child labor groups that southern cotton mill conditions were unhealthy and unsafe, especially for the children employed there. The groups were pushing for laws to protect young workers.

Stiles expanded his earlier study by comparing cotton mills in New England and the South. In his report, he wrote that he saw no severe anemia among New England mill workers. But in the South, he observed the illness in one of every eight mill workers. Employees in both northern and southern mills were breathing in cotton lint. Stiles concluded, therefore, that the so-called cotton-mill anemia in the South was largely caused by hookworm infections, not contaminated air or other working conditions.

He recommended that the mills' anemia problem could be addressed by treating hookworm-infected people and improving existing privies. Although some privies were below his standards, he declared that the overall mill conditions were healthier than on the farms.

Stiles claimed that child labor reformers were deceived about worker age. Hookworm disease made many of the infected appear several years younger and less developed than they really were. In any case, children were actually better off working in a mill than on the farm.

Stiles was so sure of himself that he publicly said "if he had to choose between placing his own 10-year-old daughter in the spinning room of a cotton mill and placing her on the average small tenant farm of the South he would be obliged in the best interests of the child to send her to the mill."

Mill owners liked his report. But his conclusion—and Stiles himself—were denounced by child labor reformers. They argued that young children did, indeed, work in the mills. The children and their parents freely admitted their ages. Stiles was wrong to say that hookworms explained all illnesses of mill workers. They suffered from long hours, poor nutrition, and dangerous conditions.

Stiles's study reflected his single-minded focus on hookworms and sanitation. He didn't attempt to diagnose any other medical causes for worker ill health. When he visited the mills, he picked out hookworm infections by the physical appearance of workers. He didn't have the time or means to confirm the disease for all victims by a microscopic examination for eggs.

Despite the shortcomings of his research, Stiles stubbornly dismissed the criticisms and stood by his conclusions.

THE TRAVELING WORM

In 1905, researchers studying hookworm disease discovered *Necator* worms in people living in West Africa. It was the first time *Necator* had been found outside the Americas.

This part of Africa was the major source of enslaved workers brought to the New World starting in the sixteenth century. The discovery suggested to Stiles and other scientists that *Necator* arrived in the Americas during this era.

Today, most biologists agree. They believe *Necator* first appeared in the subtropical and tropical areas of the New World after 1492, though it probably didn't travel here with the European explorers. That's because *Ancylostoma duodenale*—not *Necator americanus*—was the hookworm species found in Europe. *Necator* likely arrived in the bodies of Africans forced to come to the Americas as enslaved laborers.

In his 1902 survey trip, Stiles reported seeing fewer cases of hookworm disease among Black southerners than White. But neither he nor anyone else had done a careful study to determine if this was true throughout the region.

Some southern doctors told Stiles "that they had never seen a case" among the Black population. Yet Stiles received information from other physicians who said that they had observed hookworm disease in their Black patients and had verified it with microscopic tests. Stiles decided that there was "abundant evidence that such cases do occur."

In one Georgia doctor's opinion, hookworm infection among Black patients was too often overlooked. When local physicians had no microscope to check stools for hookworm eggs, they made a diagnosis using appearance alone. Based on his experience, this doctor thought that anemia was more noticeable in a White person with an abnormally pale face than it was in a Black patient. He and others pointed out that fewer Black southerners had access to healthcare or the money to pay for it. Their illnesses might not be detected by the medical community.

Another view among physicians in the South was that hookworm infection depended on living conditions rather than race. They observed more hookworm disease in patients who farmed on loose, sandy soils than in those dwelling on dense, compact ground. The residents on farms with no privies were also more likely to be infected.

During his trips, Stiles met many middle- and upper-class southerners who dismissed hookworm disease as an inevitable ailment of the poor class, not one they needed to worry about. Why should their town and state governments waste time and money on these victims? "They were not worth trying to help," one man told him.

Stiles attempted to convince people that it was important to cure everyone infected with hookworms, regardless of their income or race. No one would be truly safe from the parasite until everyone was treated and no longer spread the eggs.

He was aware of the strong racial prejudice in the early twentieth-century South. To arouse concern about hookworm among White southerners, Stiles said in his writings and speeches that Black residents were infected with hookworm and were spreading it. But they often didn't appear sick since their bodies were better adapted to the parasite and more immune to its most harmful effects. That was because of their ancestry in Africa, where *Necator* had long existed. The heritage of White southerners, however, was northern Europe, where hookworm was rare. As a result, Stiles said, they were more susceptible to *Necator*'s damage.

In the early 1900s, racial differences—actual or not—were used to motivate White southerners to fight the hookworm problem, building on their prejudice and fear of infection from Black people. Newspapers and magazines repeated Stiles's statements, arguing that poor rural White people were handicapped by hookworm disease while their Black neighbors were not. If White southerners were cured, they would become a new competent labor force to invigorate the South's economy. One journalist wrote, "The one real hope of curing the white man lies in curing the black man."

WHAT NEXT?

For six years, from 1902 to 1908, Stiles had worked to publicize America's hookworm disease epidemic. He persuaded many in the medical profession that the illness was common in their states. He spoke about the ways that the disease led to poverty and a weak economy. Yet some newspapers continued to make fun of the Lazy Germ.

Surgeon General Wyman agreed with Stiles that to eradicate the disease, more had to be done to educate the public, doctors, and local government officials. The polluting rural sanitation had to be fixed. Hundreds of thousands, probably millions, of infected southerners had to be treated. One man's effort wouldn't be enough.

A massive education and treatment effort required money. But despite lobbying by Stiles and Wyman, President Theodore Roosevelt's administration refused to authorize extra funds so that the PHS could tackle the project.

Stiles was frustrated that the federal government wouldn't support a campaign against the American Murderer. Now the only chance of launching such a program would be to raise private money. After years of fighting the parasite, Stiles wondered whether that was a realistic hope.

The Southern Curses

At the beginning of the twentieth century, the South was generally considered by the rest of the country to be an area of poor health. Hookworm wasn't the only disease that plagued rural southerners. Malaria and pellagra were widespread.

A person whose body was already weakened by one of these three ailments was at increased risk of serious illness and death from the others. People living in poverty were more susceptible to the diseases, less able to get medical care when they became sick, and more likely to die from their illness.

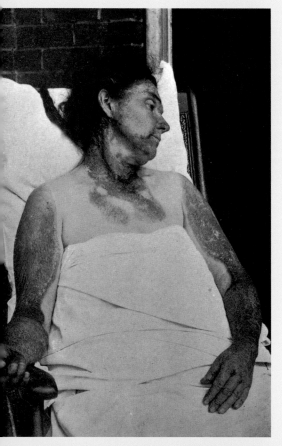

A pellagra victim in the early 1900s. The red rash and blank stare are signs of the disease. The woman also suffered from a severe mental disorder, indicating that her brain had been affected.

MALARIA

For centuries, malaria was a common disease in the United States. The symptoms include fever, chills, and fatigue. It can result in anemia and be fatal. Until the last years of the 1800s, scientists didn't realize that malaria was caused by parasitic microbes transmitted into the body by mosquitoes. Because mosquitoes breed in standing water when temperatures are warm, people were at risk if they lived or traveled near low-lying areas.

Once malaria's cause was known, efforts began to reduce mosquitoes by draining wetlands and swamps and by screening homes. But many southerners in the early 1900s remained exposed to the disease-carrying insects.

PELLAGRA

Pellagra victims experience skin rashes, diarrhea, mental disorders, and eventually, death. Although the disease had been observed in Europe since the 1700s, American doctors did not recognize pellagra in the United States until the first years of the 1900s. Most cases were in the southern states.

In 1914, medical researchers from the Public Health Service deduced that pellagra was caused by an inadequate diet. Later discoveries revealed that the key missing nutrient was the vitamin niacin. Pellagra-preventing foods, such as meat, poultry, milk, and fresh vegetables, were expensive and in short supply throughout the South during the early twentieth century. Cotton, instead of food, had taken over southern fields. The poor—including tenant farmers, sharecroppers, and mill workers—frequently lacked access to nutritious foods. More than 3 million of them developed pellagra.

When Stiles identified victims of hookworm disease based on their physical appearance alone, he likely was misdiagnosing some malnourished pellagra patients. The only way to confirm a hookworm infection was by using a microscope to see the parasite's eggs in feces.

CHAPTER SIX

"SKIDOO, HOOKWORM"

"The South is not lazy."
—*Knoxville Sentinel*

I N AUGUST 1908, CHARLES STILES HEARD THAT PRESIDENT
Roosevelt had appointed a commission to study rural life in the United States.
About one-third of the population lived on farms, and Roosevelt wanted
suggestions of ways to make farmers more prosperous. The members of the Country Life
Commission included agricultural experts, educators, and journalists.

Stiles saw the Commission as an opportunity to raise awareness about hookworm
disease. He made sure to be assigned to the group as the Public Health Service's
expert on rural sanitary conditions.

THE MAN FROM NORTH CAROLINA

One member of the Commission was Walter Page, an editor and publisher. Page
had grown up in the South. In his view, the region still hadn't recovered from the

devastation of the Civil War and the collapse of its agricultural system based on enslaved laborers.

Page thought that schooling and training lifted people from poverty. But he had seen firsthand that education was substandard in his native North Carolina, especially for Black and poor rural White residents. The South's economy wasn't strong enough to support schools the way communities in the North and West did. Page was eager to help the Commission determine how to change that situation.

The Commission members traveled together by train throughout the United States, meeting with rural groups to learn about their problems and to discuss solutions. During their tour of the South, Stiles became friendly with Page and another Commission member, Iowan Henry Wallace Sr., who was the editor of an agriculture magazine.

At daybreak one morning in November 1908, the three men were sitting together when the train stopped at a small country station in eastern North Carolina.

Through the window, Wallace noticed a gaunt, ashen man standing on the station platform. The man looked half-dead. Aware that Page had been raised in the state, Wallace asked what in the world was wrong with the fellow.

Page told him that such a person was known as a dirt-eater. He added that the pathetic man was likely one of the tenant farmers, "a so-called 'poor white.'"

Wallace was appalled. No Iowan farmer looked this withered and weak. In fact, Wallace had never seen anyone like this. "If he represents Southern farm labor the South is in poor luck," he said.

Walter Page (1855–1918)
Born in North Carolina, Page grew up during the Civil War watching the businesses of his father and others ruined by the conflict. After attending college in North Carolina, Virginia, and Maryland, he worked as a journalist in Missouri. In 1882, Page returned to North Carolina and founded a newspaper in Raleigh. Soon after, he went to Boston and New York City to write for major national periodicals, later becoming editor of the *World's Work* magazine and partner in the book publisher Doubleday, Page & Company. From 1913 to 1918, Page served as America's ambassador to Great Britain, a period that included World War I.

Stiles spotted the emaciated man on the platform, too. He had met thousands of similar rural southerners and was certain this man had been heavily infected with hookworms for a long time. Stiles explained to the others that they were looking at a case of hookworm disease.

"Can that man be cured?" Page asked.

"About fifty cents worth of drugs will completely cure him," replied Stiles. He knew this, he said, because he'd seen it happen with countless hookworm victims.

INSULTED

Walter Page had read about Stiles's Lazy Germ. He wasn't alone in not taking it seriously—until now. Could hookworms explain the condition of so many people he had seen in North Carolina since his boyhood?

Stiles was always ready to share the details, just as he had many times during the previous six years. He told Page and Wallace that at least 2 million southerners of all ages were victims of hookworm. He discussed how they became infected and shared his ideas for eradicating the parasite.

Later that day the Country Life Commission hosted a public hearing in Raleigh, North Carolina's capital. During the meeting, Page brought up hookworms. He asked a local doctor about the extent of hookworm disease in North Carolina.

"I have never seen a case here," the physician replied.

Stiles couldn't let such an ignorant comment pass. "There are four well-marked cases of hookworm in this room at the present moment," he interjected. He informed the audience that North Carolina children were anemic and "below the standard of healthy children in other parts of the country."

His reply shocked the audience. The next day it made the newspapers.

Raleigh's *News and Observer* was scathing. It contended that if the Commission wanted to do good in the state, it should learn about the

Willie Livingston, age nineteen, lived in Mississippi. He only weighed 109 pounds (49 kg) and was so weak that he could barely walk. Those who knew him thought he was near death. After three thymol treatments over a period of three weeks, he was hookworm-free. Willie gained 18 pounds (8 kg) and recovered his energy. Cases like this convinced Stiles that a large, hookworm campaign could dramatically improve the health of millions of infected southerners.

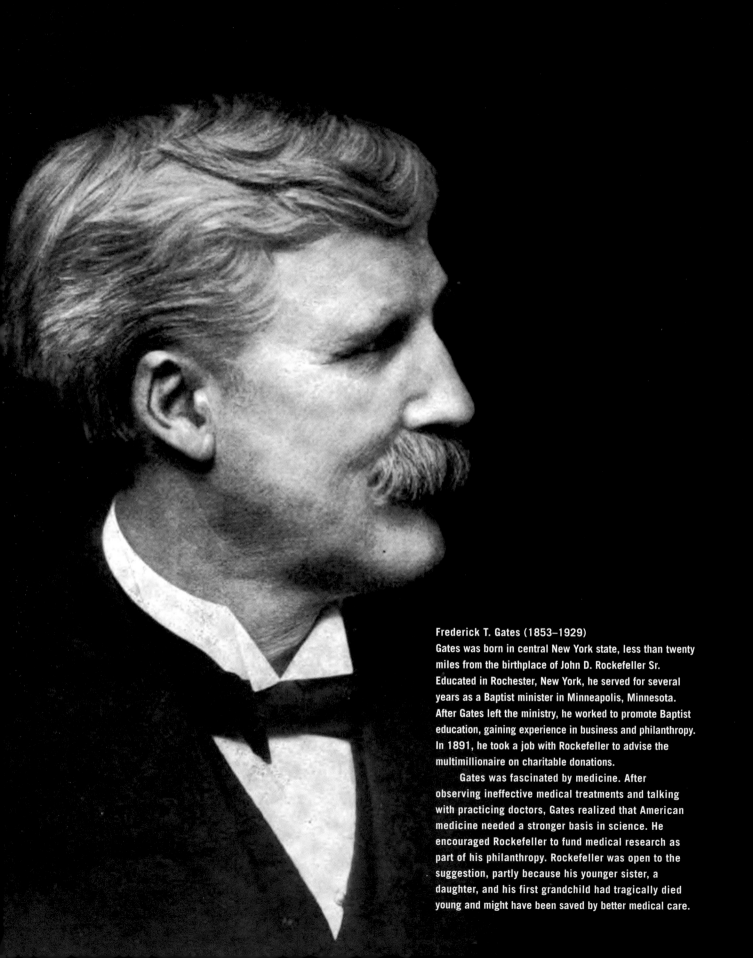

Frederick T. Gates (1853–1929)
Gates was born in central New York state, less than twenty miles from the birthplace of John D. Rockefeller Sr. Educated in Rochester, New York, he served for several years as a Baptist minister in Minneapolis, Minnesota. After Gates left the ministry, he worked to promote Baptist education, gaining experience in business and philanthropy. In 1891, he took a job with Rockefeller to advise the multimillionaire on charitable donations.

Gates was fascinated by medicine. After observing ineffective medical treatments and talking with practicing doctors, Gates realized that American medicine needed a stronger basis in science. He encouraged Rockefeller to fund medical research as part of his philanthropy. Rockefeller was open to the suggestion, partly because his younger sister, a daughter, and his first grandchild had tragically died young and might have been saved by better medical care.

real problems, such as "a bad tenant system, . . . the lack of health facilities and schools, and the employment of children in factories" and not "broadcast preconceived notions" about hookworms. The newspaper's editorial said, "The Country Life Commission has left a distinctly bad taste in the mouths of our people."

North Carolina's governor condemned Stiles and the Commission for the insult. The comments "had more of the appearance of being an attempt to injure the State than to improve it." The governor accused them of misrepresenting the "true conditions" in North Carolina.

The newspaper and governor also called out Walter Page. Page was angry that they unfairly accused him of "slandering the land of my birth!"

Stiles ignored the attacks. He knew his warnings had awakened many southern doctors to the existence of the parasite and shown them how to look for it. And they had found it.

As Walter Page heard more about Stiles's research and the methods of preventing and curing hookworm disease, he realized its importance. If southerners could be free of the disease and have more energy to work and study, Page was convinced they could rise from poverty. The region's economy would benefit.

Page had connections to many prominent people. Through his contacts, he put Stiles in touch with Frederick T. Gates, who worked for the multimillionaire owner of Standard Oil, John D. Rockefeller. Gates had managed Rockefeller's philanthropic giving for seventeen years, and Page thought Rockefeller might be interested in the hookworm problem.

The timing was right.

CHARITY

The Rockefeller family had already embarked on a major program to help the South. During a 1901 train tour of the region, Rockefeller's son, John Jr., discovered that illiteracy was significantly higher among southerners than in the rest of the country, particularly among Black people. Was there a way to change that?

With Gates's assistance, the Rockefellers created the General Education Board (GEB) in 1903. Through the GEB, they contributed tens of millions of dollars to improve primary and secondary instruction as well as to support technical and professional schools in the southern states. Walter Page was a member of the GEB board.

Because communities needed taxes to run their schools, the GEB recognized that rural economies had to be stronger than they were. That required an increase in farm production. Part of the Board's focus was helping farmers learn better agricultural methods so that they could produce more crops and earn more income.

Gates saw that hookworm disease could undermine the GEB's efforts with southern farmers. He asked several medical experts about Stiles and hookworm. Who was this scientist? Was the Lazy Germ really the joke the newspapers made it out to be?

One of them told Gates, "If Doctor Stiles believes this, it is something to be taken most seriously."

Reports from others assured Gates that Stiles was respected for his knowledge. He invited the scientist to come to New York and provide more details about his hookworm work.

Stiles arrived at Gates's office armed with his photographs and drawings. He even had a microscope and specimens of the parasite. Gates was impressed. Stiles, Gates recalled, "offered conclusive proofs. He showed the worms, disclosed their hooks, and exhibited visually the complete cycle of their life history."

Gates asked Stiles to estimate the number of people with hookworm disease in the United States.

"Perhaps two million cases in the South," Stiles told him, repeating the number he'd given Walter Page during their train tour. He added that this was only a guess based on his southern travels because no formal count had ever been done.

Although hookworm disease was common in the South, Stiles said, it could be treated easily and cheaply. Proper sanitation would prevent it from recurring. Ashford's clinics in Puerto Rico had demonstrated that a hookworm campaign reduced infections and anemia. Stiles was confident that the parasite could be eliminated, maybe for $500,000.

THE GIFT

Gates came away convinced that a campaign to eradicate hookworm disease was a cause worthy of the Rockefellers' attention. It complemented other Rockefeller programs, including medical research and the General Education Board. In fact, the GEB's goals were doomed if hookworm-infected adults were too weak to work and their children were too sick to attend school. The disease trapped families and communities in poverty, damaging the economic vitality of the region.

John D. Rockefeller never met Stiles or heard his worm presentation. But Gates had been persuaded, and that was enough for both Rockefellers—father and son. They agreed to donate $1 million (the equivalent of about $29 million today).

The program would be called the Rockefeller Sanitary Commission for the Eradication of Hookworm Disease, shortened to the Rockefeller Sanitary Commission, or RSC. The Commission's task was to set up a hookworm campaign that combined the efforts of doctors, public health officials, churches, schools, businesses, and the press.

Before the gift was publicly announced, Gates wanted everything in place. He had read criticisms of Stiles's declaration that the parasite infected millions of southerners. Gates realized that many in the South were sensitive about the subject. For the hookworm eradication project to succeed, it couldn't appear to be the work of a group of northerners pointing out the South's faults and trying to fix them.

With that in mind, Gates set up the Commission's offices in Washington, a neutral city, rather than in New York where the Rockefeller headquarters were located.

Understanding that success depended on southerners respecting the people who managed the program, Gates invited several well-known leaders from the South to join the Commission's board of directors. These included physicians, scientists, and educators. Gates arranged for Stiles to speak to the group.

After hearing Stiles's graphic hookworm presentation, everyone agreed to join the board. They "immediately recognized the mysterious 'ground itch' of their barefoot boyhood," Gates later wrote. Thanks to Stiles, they now knew that hookworm had caused it. "They saw in its eradication a new hope for the South."

Walter Page was pleased when Gates asked him to be part of the Sanitary Commission. "It is the largest single benefit that could be done to the people of the South," he said.

Gates also invited Stiles to be a member of the Commission's board. Stiles had finally brought attention and funding to the medical problem to which he'd devoted himself for years. "This gift is one of the grandest acts of Mr. Rockefeller's life," he told a reporter. "It means . . . a reduction of the death rate, better results from educational efforts, and greater happiness and health to hundreds of thousands of people."

Once Gates had organized the twelve-member board of directors, with himself as its chairman, he was ready to go public with news of the Commission. On October 26, 1909, John D. Rockefeller Sr. sent a letter to the new board members. In it, he pledged funds for a five-year "aggressive campaign, up to a total of One Million Dollars" to control hookworm disease in the southern states.

The letter explained that Rockefeller wished to relieve suffering and, in particular, to help southerners. He had become familiar with the region and "its warm-hearted people" while spending winter vacations in Georgia. This financial gift was his way of thanking them for "their many kindnesses and hospitalities."

Gates arranged for the letter to appear in newspapers across the country.

Newspapers around the nation reported on Rockefeller's $1 million gift to fight hookworm disease in the South. Some continued to call hookworm the "Lazy Bug." This appeared in the *Washington Post*, October 29, 1909.

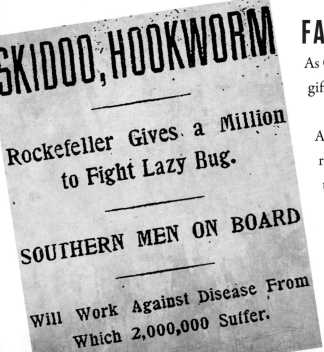

SKIDOO, HOOKWORM

Rockefeller Gives a Million to Fight Lazy Bug.

SOUTHERN MEN ON BOARD

Will Work Against Disease From Which 2,000,000 Suffer.

FALLOUT

As Gates feared, the southern response to Rockefeller's $1 million gift wasn't all positive.

Some newspapers did welcome the new program. An Alabama newspaper noted that the hookworm problem was real, hundreds of cases had been diagnosed and treated, and the states didn't have the funds to carry on such a campaign. The choice, the newspaper said, was "the states doing the work themselves, letting Mr. Rockefeller's money do it for them, or permitting conditions, known to be serious, to remain as they are."

South Is Able to Eradicate Its Own Worms, Says Bishop Candler

But many newspaper editorials expressed resentment toward the do-gooders and press in the North. "The South is represented to be filled with a wretched brood of dirt-eaters. Who that knows the South can for a moment believe this?"

A Tennessee newspaper argued that Stiles's estimate of 2 million southerners being infected with hookworm was much exaggerated. Rockefeller might have meant well by donating a million dollars to fight the parasite, it went on, "but the incident will no doubt serve further to accentuate the notion already lodged in so many Northern craniums that the Southern whites are lazy. . . . The South is not lazy."

One businessman voiced his objection to the way the South was portrayed. "Uncleanliness is no more common below Mason and Dixon's line than it is in the North or West."

A frequent comment was that Rockefeller was wasting his money. The poor and anemic were like that because they were lazy and weren't motivated to work. "There is less hookworm in the South than inherent no-accountness. . . . All the millions of Congress will not help those who will not help themselves."

The prominent leader of the Baptist Church, Bishop Warren Candler, wrote to a Georgia newspaper, "This habit of singling out the South for all sorts of reforms, remedies, and enlightenment is not for our benefit. . . . Mr. Rockefeller would take charge of both our heads and our stomachs, and purge our brains of ignorance and our bowels of worms." His letter was published in many other southern newspapers.

A rumor circulated in the South that Rockefeller's true goal was to frighten people into wearing shoes because he planned to invest in the shoe business.

Gates sensed that the RSC's work wasn't going to be easy. And a crucial position still needed to be filled—the person who would head the Commission and manage the program day-to-day. To deal with southern resentment, the choice had to be made with great care.

Many southerners took offense at Rockefeller's funding of the Sanitary Commission for the Eradication of Hookworm Disease. Headline from the *Macon* [GA] *Daily Telegraph*, November 3, 1909

Charles Stiles was the hookworm expert and the first to notice and publicize the epidemic. He likely expected to lead this campaign against the parasite.

But Frederick Gates was aware of Stiles's arrogance toward country doctors and his blunt insensitivity with the public. In one newspaper interview, Stiles told a reporter, "Most of the rural schools and churches are a disgrace to the South, and to the country at large." He went on to say that they were "dangerous agents in carrying the hookworm disease." Besides that, Stiles's comments about the cotton mills had outraged the powerful child labor reformers. Gates knew the RSC wouldn't succeed if any of these groups were antagonized.

He decided that Stiles's role should be limited to representing the Commission with the medical and scientific communities, not the press and public. Stiles would act as the group's scientific advisor while maintaining his job with the Public Health Service.

Gates and the board members chose a Tennessee college professor and dean, Wickliffe Rose, to lead the RSC. Rose was respected in southern education circles, people who were essential in bringing attention to hookworm disease. Rose also possessed two important character traits that Charles Stiles lacked—modesty and tactfulness.

Rose turned out to be perfect for the job.

Wickliffe Rose (1862–1931)
Born in Tennessee, Rose was a professor
of philosophy and history as well as a
college dean in Nashville. He was active
in organizations dedicated to improving
public education in the South. In
December 1909, he became administrative
secretary of the Rockefeller Sanitary
Commission. Rose later worked with the
Rockefeller Foundation on health and
education issues until his retirement.

John D. Rockefeller

John Davison Rockefeller Sr. (1839–1937) and his son, John D. Rockefeller Jr. (1874–1960) in 1921

One of six children, John Davison Rockefeller was born in the village of Richford in central New York. During John's childhood, the family moved from town to town in that region. In 1853, his father took the family to Cleveland, Ohio. At sixteen, John entered the business world when he became a clerk at a small Cleveland shipping company.

After the first American oil well was drilled in Titusville, Pennsylvania, in 1859, refineries popped up throughout that area, including around Cleveland. Rockefeller invested in one of them in 1863. He was shrewd and hardworking, and as the oil industry grew, his business did, too. In 1870, he formed Standard Oil. Within a few years, the company owned nearly all of America's refineries and pipelines. Rockefeller was soon one of the wealthiest men in the world.

In 1902, journalist Ida Tarbell wrote a series of articles for *McClure's Magazine* about the history of Standard Oil. Her series was published as a book in 1904. Americans read about the ways Rockefeller built his oil monopoly by destroying his rivals, often using unethical means.

Public hostility toward Rockefeller grew in reaction to his business practices. His products touched everyone. All Americans had to buy their lighting kerosene (an oil product) from Rockefeller, and with no competition, they were forced to pay whatever price he charged.

In March 1911, the U.S. Supreme Court agreed with lower courts that Standard Oil unfairly interfered with trade. The Court ruled that Standard Oil must be dissolved into thirty separate companies. But as Rockefeller kept making money from his many companies, the controversy and criticism continued.

An illustration from *Puck* magazine, February 27, 1901, shows John D. Rockefeller Sr. as a king wearing a crown of oil wells, refineries, and railroad companies—all part of Standard Oil. He was harshly criticized for the monopoly control he had over the oil industry.

THE GOSPEL ACCORDING TO "ST. JOHN."

The illustration called "The Gospel according to 'St. John,'" from *Puck* magazine, May 3, 1905, points out the two sides of Rockefeller: the religious philanthropist and the businessman who squeezes people by forcing them to pay high prices for his oil.

THE DUTY TO GIVE

Rockefeller was instilled with strong religious principles by his mother. He believed that God was the source of his success, and he had the responsibility to donate part of his earnings to the needy. Beginning in his teens, he gave to charities throughout his life. At first, most of the recipients were church-related, especially the Baptist Church of which he was a member. As he amassed more money, he broadened the scope of his donations.

Besieged by thousands of requests for money (at times, more than fifty thousand a month), Rockefeller became overwhelmed by reviewing them and deciding on the worthiest. In 1891, he hired Frederick Gates to assist him.

Besides funding the hookworm disease campaign, Rockefeller financed education, including the University of Chicago and Spelman College, an Atlanta school for Black women. The college was named after his wife, Laura Spelman, and her parents, who had been active in the antislavery movement before the Civil War. He also established the Rockefeller Institute for Medical Research (known today as Rockefeller University).

In 1913, with Gates's encouragement, Rockefeller combined several separate philanthropic groups under the umbrella of the Rockefeller Foundation to continue donations in the United States and throughout the world.

Rockefeller and his wife had five children. His only son, John D. Rockefeller Jr., joined the family business and philanthropies in 1897.

CHAPTER SEVEN

HOOKWORM SOCIALS

"The scenes at these dispensaries . . .
are in a high degree interesting and thrilling."
—Frederick Gates

WHEN WICKLIFFE ROSE ACCEPTED THE JOB OF RUNNING the RSC, he knew what Gates and Rockefeller had in mind. Most of the southern states lacked well-developed public health agencies. The RSC would help to build up these systems while fighting the hookworm epidemic. After the Commission and its money ended in five years, each state was expected to take responsibility for its own hookworm program.

ON THE FRONT LINES

Stiles had already convinced health leaders in eleven southern states that they had a hookworm problem. They asked the Rockefeller Sanitary Commission to help them solve it. During 1910, Rose traveled to each participating state to set up its program.

The RSC and the state's health officials jointly appointed a sanitation director to oversee the hookworm campaign. This person was usually a doctor on the state board of health who had experience treating patients, working in public health, and doing lab work.

The new director chose three to six assistants, called sanitary inspectors, to travel throughout the state and meet with local doctors and the public. Most were recent medical school graduates in their twenties or early thirties. All were White men. Knowing how southerners felt about northern interference in their affairs, Rose required the inspectors to have been raised and educated in the South.

The state's board of health paid the sanitary inspectors' salaries with funds provided by the RSC. Rose urged the states to be the face of the hookworm campaign. To keep Rockefeller and the Commission behind the scenes, Rose didn't give newspaper interviews about any state's activities.

The RSC recognized that controlling hookworm disease required local physicians to identify and treat people in their communities. "The task is enormous; it will require years for its accomplishment," Rose wrote in the 1910 Commission report. "It will be done only by the doctors working intelligently, patiently, persistently, each in his own territory."

Despite Stiles's efforts, many southern doctors were still unfamiliar with hookworm disease and failed to spot its symptoms in their patients. Others doubted the disease was serious enough to worry about. For the campaign to work, these physicians had to be educated.

The sanitary inspectors built relationships with local physicians and county health officials. Each state board of health sent information to their state's doctors explaining how to diagnose hookworm disease, how to treat it, and how the parasite spread. Charles Stiles, acting as the RSC scientific advisor, supplied the facts for these materials.

The states participating in the Rockefeller Sanitary Commission's hookworm campaign:

Alabama
Arkansas
Georgia
Kentucky
Louisiana
Mississippi
North Carolina
South Carolina
Tennessee
Texas (eastern counties only)
Virginia

(Florida didn't join the other states because its board of health already operated a hookworm campaign.)

Fieldworkers, including sanitary inspectors and microscopists, traveled to remote rural areas on horseback in North Carolina (top) and by wagon on dirt roads in Kentucky (bottom). Occasionally, a suspicious backwoods resident threatened the visitors with a gun. The fieldworkers won them over with friendly conversation, photographs, and a microscope.

State directors and Commission members lectured at medical schools and meetings of physicians. In the RSC's first year, Stiles alone gave 246 speeches about hookworm disease. Gradually, more and more southern doctors began to accept that the disease existed in their communities.

By the end of the first year, Rose and Gates were satisfied with the progress the RSC was making. Gates reported back to John D. Rockefeller Sr. that the hookworm program was a success so far. "It looks as though we had hit on one of the great world miseries and that this movement is destined to be world wide before we get through with it."

WHERE ARE THE WORMS?

The Commission's strategy for eradicating hookworm was devised mainly by Gates, Rose, and Stiles. First, the RSC would determine where hookworm disease existed— by county—in the eleven southern states. Then the Commission would estimate how many of the 24 million individuals in those states were affected. Second, infected people would be treated and cured. Finally, the infection's source had to be eliminated in order to prevent future hookworm disease. That meant stopping soil pollution.

To accomplish the first goal, each state director sent letters to his state's doctors, requesting that they report hookworm cases they'd seen and treated. To gather additional data, the sanitary inspectors in the field surveyed counties by examining a sample of the population.

Although Stiles claimed he could diagnose hookworm disease by a patient's physical appearance, the inspectors relied on microscopic evidence of hookworm eggs in feces. Using RSC funds, each state's board of health paid for the training and salaries of field microscopists. Other members of the team included microscopists and technicians stationed at the state health laboratory, who also examined fecal samples sent there by the doctors.

By the end of December 1911, the RSC compiled the information and calculated that at least 2 million southerners carried hookworms. People of all ages and all social and economic classes were infected.

A study in North Carolina sampled more than 5,000 people and found 43 percent infected. Alabama, Georgia, and South Carolina also had infection rates between 40 and 50 percent of their populations. In a few states, every county had hookworm cases. In many rural schools, all the children were infected. Some of those who had dismissed Stiles's earlier claims, including several newspaper editors, finally acknowledged the hookworm problem.

A curious group surrounds two field microscopists in Mississippi.

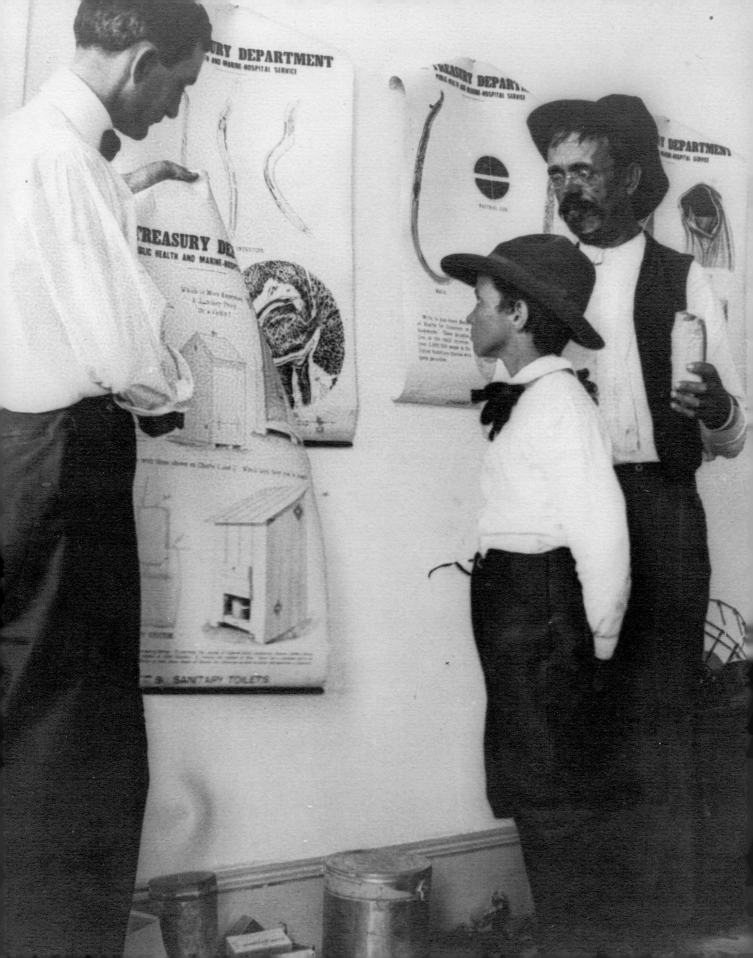

TREATING THE INFECTED

The RSC's second goal was to cure the infected. Before sanitary inspectors could accomplish this, they had to convince people that hookworms were truly a danger. Many southerners didn't believe hookworms existed. After all, they couldn't see the parasite. They resented the suggestion that they were infested with worms, and they resisted being examined or treated.

To prove that hookworms were real, the sanitary inspectors gave talks to community groups—churches, women's clubs, county officials, schools. The doctors used everyday, unscientific language to describe the parasite's life cycle and the symptoms of hookworm disease.

People were invited to look at photographs of the adult worms and peer through a microscope to see the eggs and larvae. The inspectors explained that hookworm spread through soil pollution and that the familiar ground itch was an ominous sign of the American Murderer invading the body. They told how the infection was easily cured with thymol.

By speaking with local leaders, ministers, teachers, and doctors, a sanitary inspector learned who in the community might have symptoms of hookworm disease. Then he and a microscopist stopped by the home for a visit.

The inspector showed his bottles of adult hookworms so that people saw what might be causing their ill health. If the microscopist found hookworm eggs in a stool sample, the inspector encouraged the family to be treated with thymol, preferably by their doctor. But when they didn't have one, he administered the treatment. The next step was discussing how the family could prevent reinfection by improving their sanitation and wearing shoes.

Some sanitary inspectors photographed a patient before treatment and a few weeks later. They displayed these pictures when they visited others. People were stunned by the visible change, and they often agreed to be treated, too.

A state sanitary inspector in Alabama uses posters to explain hookworms and proper privy construction. People were advised to build a sanitary privy and to wear shoes. If they couldn't afford shoes, they were told to avoid infected areas after rain or dew.

As a southerner, Wickliffe Rose was aware of the region's racism, and he didn't want this prejudice to influence the Sanitary Commission's work. The inspectors examined and treated people of all races, and the RSC's statistics and records didn't indicate a patient's race. Rose wrote to the head of the Alabama State Board of Health, "One of the fine things about this to me is that the work has been done without any suggestion of race distinction."

Yet because of segregation in the South at this time, the organizations and schools that the field team visited were always separated by race.

MOBILIZING THE PRESS

In June 1911, Rose went into the field with one of the Virginia sanitary inspectors to see for himself how the program was working. The inspector and his team had spent a year treating cases and educating people about the disease. They had surveyed school-age children in the county and found that more than eight of ten were heavily infected with hookworms.

Rose traveled with the inspector to visit several families. He met parents whose children had died from severe anemia. The families had lost hope that life could be better. But after the inspector treated them, the adults were working and the surviving children were attending school.

"The results which I witnessed here are not only gratifying, they are stirring," Rose wrote to Frederick Gates. "I predict that within five years the whole face of the country in those pockets of extreme infection will be changed and one will see here a new people and a new earth."

But to make that happen, the campaign had to reach more southerners. Rose understood that the press was important in shaping public attitudes. The RSC and state directors contacted newspaper editors, sending them articles and asking them to publish the material as a public service. The relentless push paid off.

Southern newspapers printed full-page features about hookworm disease, including its cause and cure. Vivid descriptions of emaciation, bloating, cravings, exhaustion, and stunted growth grabbed the attention of southerners who recognized these symptoms in themselves or their families.

"Many children have become pale and are stunted and dwarfed both in mind and body by this disease," said one Tennessee newspaper article, "and it has made chronic invalids of a great many adults."

The articles often used scare tactics. Large drawings of the parasite sucking blood from the intestine wall were enough to create nightmares. A 1912 Mississippi newspaper article left one young reader with the memory of "a bloodcurdling illustration of a greatly enlarged female hookworm that resembled a diamondback rattlesnake more than a worm" and the "emaciated boy teetering on the brink of the grave."

The consequences of ignoring hookworm disease were grim. Articles warned that a victim was unlikely to resist fatal diseases like tuberculosis and pneumonia.

Stories about actual victims provided proof that even the most hopeless case could be cured. Before-and-after photographs of hookworm patients showed the benefits of the healing treatment—a healthy body and a happy family.

The state boards of health printed free pamphlets, distributing thousands each year to their citizens. Pamphlets contained basic information about hookworm disease, often in question-and-answer format. Included were drawings of the parasite and sanitary privies.

A pamphlet distributed by the Alabama Board of Health featured a photograph of a barefoot family of seven. The caption identified them all as being severely infected with hookworm, adding, "Three children have died. The cost of three lives and three funerals is the price this family paid because they had no privy."

THE DISPENSARIES

In December 1911, a sanitary inspector in Columbia, Mississippi, tried a new way of drawing in the public to be examined, treated, and educated about hookworm disease. He persuaded the county health office to donate space so that he could set up a dispensary, a term used to describe a free medical clinic.

County officials supplied money to buy medicine and to advertise the hookworm dispensary hours. The sanitary inspector recruited local physicians to assist with patients. He added hookworm displays, microscopes, and an examination area.

Some of the people who attended this Mississippi dispensary pose for the camera. On this day, 247 people were treated.

The microscopists and technicians were responsible for spotting hookworm eggs and dead adults in stool samples. Some states hired women to perform this work, paying them less than the men. These women are working at a Kentucky dispensary set up in a hotel lobby. A hookworm poster hangs on the wall among the hotel's usual artwork. Stiles and the PHS supplied many of the informational charts and posters.

When people heard that they could be tested and treated for free, they flocked to the dispensary. During nearly five months, 1,000 were treated—far more than the field team had been able to help before. Other Mississippi counties tried the dispensaries, too, and treated thousands of people during the next several months.

Wickliffe Rose saw the free dispensaries as an effective way to reach people who couldn't afford a doctor. He suggested that the other states do the same. But the RSC wouldn't allow the fieldworkers to run a dispensary unless the county government paid some of the costs, usually the medicine and advertising. It was important to Rockefeller and Gates that local communities commit to the hookworm campaign.

Throughout the South, field teams set up temporary dispensaries in schools, courthouses, hotels, and even on the sides of roads. One or more inspectors operated four or five dispensaries in a county, getting local physicians to help out. The doctors visited each location one day a week for a period of several weeks.

The county advertised the location and days for each site, using newspapers, mailings, and public notices. The fieldworkers enlisted ministers, teachers, and

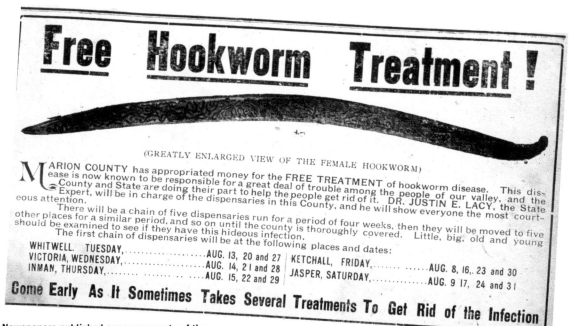

Newspapers published announcements of the free dispensaries. This one from the *Sequachee Valley* [TN] *News* includes the clinic times and locations along with an eye-catching drawing of a female hookworm.

The dispensaries were social affairs. Families came early and stayed all day, often wearing their best clothes. The Lovett family of Alabama pose for a photo after being treated at a county dispensary. All of them had heavy infections. Seventy percent of schoolchildren in their county carried hookworms.

community leaders to encourage attendance. One newspaper urged its readers to go: "It means health for you and your children, and greater prosperity and happiness in the years to come."

People were told to bring a small amount of their feces to be examined for hookworm eggs by a microscopist. Public officials brought their own stool samples to the dispensaries, too. When the governor of Kentucky did this, he made sure the newspapers covered the story.

People came from miles around, traveling by horse or foot. Families dressed in their best clothes, climbed in their wagon or buggy, and drove as far as twenty miles. In Mississippi, three small boys appeared every week at their county's dispensary, each saddled on a young bull.

The sanitary inspector engaged the crowd by showing photographs, posters, and hookworm specimens. Because some dispensary visitors—adults and children—couldn't read, these visual aids helped to get the message across. He explained the thymol treatment and asked people who had been cured to come forward and speak to the crowd about their experience.

The dispensaries turned into entertaining get-togethers. Visitors frequently brought lunch and stayed all day to socialize with friends and neighbors. At times, the groups sang church songs.

NORTH CAROLINA STATE MEDICAL DISPENSARY FOR THE FREE TREATMENT OF THE HOOKWORM DISEASE.

DR. PLATT W. COVINGTON IN CHARGE. F. W. CONNOR, MICROSCOPIST.

DIRECTIONS TO PATIENT.

At night, after supper, take a large dose of Epsom Salts. Eat no breakfast the following morning. Instead, take one-half of all the Capsules at 6 a. m., the others at 8 a. m., and at 10 a. m. take a full size dose of Salts. Lie on right side for 30 minutes after taking capsules. It is DANGEROUS to take anything except water while the capsules are in the body. A light dinner may be eaten after the last dose of salts acts well.

If either dose of Salts fails to act well, take another and larger one.

A PRIZE OF THREE DOLLARS WILL BE GIVEN TO THE ONE WHO RETURNS TO THE DISPENSARY WITH THE LARGEST NUMBER OF WORMS IN A BOTTLE.

This card came from a North Carolina dispensary. When someone's stool contained hookworm eggs, he or she was given free thymol and Epsom salts with instructions on how to take them at home. People were told to strain their feces through a thin cloth after the treatment, collect the worms, and return them to the dispensary in a bottle. The person who brought back the most worms won a prize.

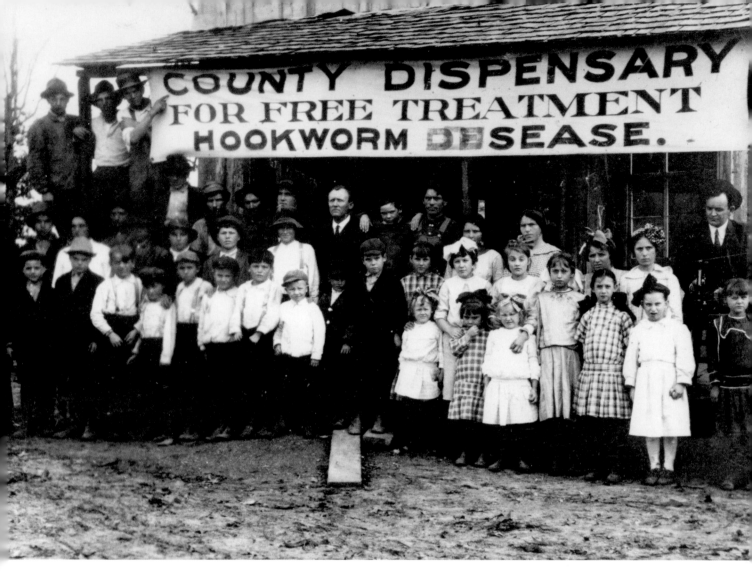

Visitors to an Alabama free county dispensary pose with the three men (wearing ties) who ran it. The man on the right holds a microscope used to examine the stool samples people brought with them.

SUCCESS STORIES

Rose was pleased when he read the sanitary inspectors' reports to the state directors. In some counties, more than half the residents had come to a dispensary. The field doctors discovered hookworms in children as young as three months and in adults as old as ninety-four.

Thousands of people showed up at one Kentucky dispensary held on the lawn of the county courthouse. All the local doctors participated. The sanitary inspector wrote, "We have had a total of 881 specimens brought in. The entire county is greatly aroused."

Every member of the Beevers family of Louisiana was heavily infected before their thymol treatment. In their county, more than 2,000 other people were examined at dispensaries, and 60 percent of them had hookworm infections.

Stories about cured patients inspired Rose and the rest of the Commission's board of directors. One eleven-year-old boy, sickly and weak, had been treated for four years by twelve different doctors. Nothing helped. After receiving thymol, the child rapidly recovered his strength and put on weight.

A carpenter, age twenty-six, had suffered for five years, becoming so exhausted that he could only work a few hours a day. After his hookworm treatment, he regained his energy and was working full-time again at good wages.

Before hearing about the dispensaries, Dave Yates and his Tennessee family of ten had spent more than $1500 over several years on useless quack medicines to cure their ailments. Microscopic examinations revealed that they all were severely infected with hookworms. The thymol treatments finally made the family healthy again.

Often a person gained a pound a week after the hookworms were gone. These results amazed the victims, their families, and the neighbors. When others saw the change in appearance and energy, they were eager to visit a dispensary and be tested.

The dispensaries became more than places to treat the poor for hookworm. They even attracted people who could afford to see a physician. Importantly, the dispensaries were an effective way to educate everyone in the community about hookworm.

The Rockefeller Sanitary Commission was on its way to accomplishing its three goals. But the most challenging one remained. Stopping the spread of hookworm forever.

NOTICE!

The State Board of Health, acting with Columbus County will open a field hospital for the treatment of HOOKWORM and other such diseases, at the following places in the county, on the dates named below:

Chadbourn, July 10th to 16th.
Whiteville, July 17th to 23rd.
Fair Bluff, July 24th to 30th.
Tabor, August 1st to 7th.
Lake Waccamaw, August 6th to 14th.
Freeman, August 14th to 21st.

There will be two wards in this hospital, one for males and one for females. A physician from the State Board of Health will be in charge of the hospital and an expert from the State Laboratory of Hygiene will be present to do the microscopic work.

A lady chaperone will be in charge of the female ward and every courtesy and attention will be given all persons, rich or poor.

There will be illustrated lectures and demonstrations on sanitation daily. These will be in plain simple terms that any one can understand and any one can also see the workings of that wonderful instrument, the microscope, by simply asking the man in charge. We want every man, woman and child to be examined while the hospital is in his or her section.

Many of the bad feelings people have, are due to hookworm and we have found that about half of the people are infected.

This is Absolutely FREE---The State and County Are Paying For It.

So many people have been found infected and the results are so certain and so wonderful that the County and the State feel that it is worth dollars and cents to them to restore so many of their people to health and strength.

Come out on the dates named and see what is being done. Don't think it is the other fellow who needs this. It may be you. Bring a small bit of your bowel movement with you to be examined with the microscope. It may be worth many dollars or may be life itself to you or your child. You will have only this one chance for free treatment.

Respectfully,

DR. C. L. PRIDGEN, State Board of Health.

Public notices informed county residents of upcoming hookworm dispensaries. This one from North Carolina emphasizes that the treatment is free and the results are "certain" and "wonderful." The notice makes no mention of the Rockefeller Sanitary Commission, but the RSC was the force behind it.

Victims Cured

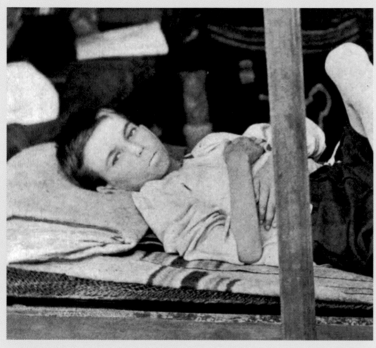

In July 1911, Selma Ellis was brought into a county dispensary on a stretcher. The North Carolinian was so weak that he couldn't walk or even sit up. No one thought he would live much longer.

Although Selma was sixteen, he had the body of a child. He weighed 62 pounds (28 kg) and was only 4 feet, 7 inches tall (1.4 m). His family said that he'd been ill and lethargic for half his life. He wasn't able to work or go to school.

In the photograph above, Selma lies on a cot at the dispensary. Doctors checked his feces and found many hookworm eggs. Diagnosed with severe hookworm disease, Selma was initially treated at the temporary dispensary until it closed. Because his treatment wasn't finished, he was moved to the PHS Marine Hospital in Wilmington, North Carolina.

Charles Stiles completed the treatment there until Selma passed no more hookworm eggs or adults. The teen had been infected with several hundred parasites. Stiles later called it "the most severe case of hookworm disease I have ever seen."

The photograph on the right shows Selma after seven weeks of treatment. He had gained 17 pounds (8 kg) and could run. For the first time, he was strong enough to go to school. While still small for his age, his body was beginning to recover from hookworm disease.

Many southern newspapers printed Selma's story and photographs to illustrate how hookworm treatment could change a life. In September 1912, Charles Stiles took Selma to an American Public Health Association conference in Washington to demonstrate the success of the RSC program.

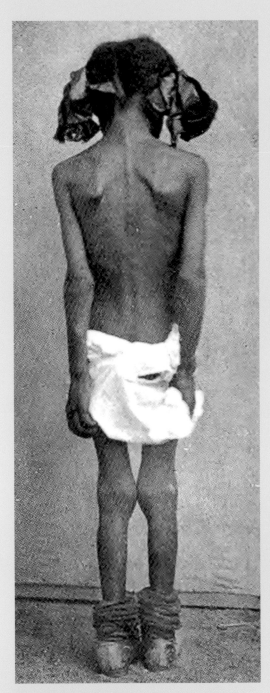

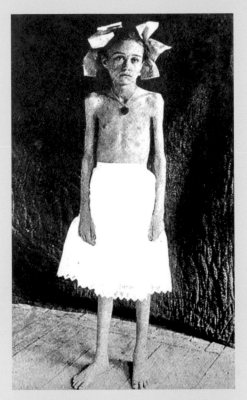

Lena Bell Tolan, of Arkansas, was eleven when her parents brought her to a free dispensary. She weighed only 33 pounds (15 kg). Her shoulder blades protruded, her body was emaciated, and she was far behind in physical maturity. Lena was examined, found to be infected with hookworms, and treated successfully with thymol.

Della Carder, an Arkansas sixteen-year-old, looked like a child of seven or eight in the photograph on the top. During the course of several years, doctors had treated her for malaria and tuberculosis. The real cause of her health problems was hookworms. After treatment, Della's health and normal growth quickly returned.

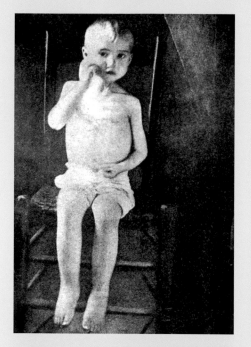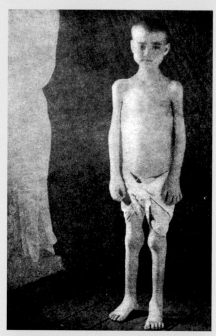

In the top photographs, these Kentucky brothers show symptoms of severe hookworm disease—emaciated body, blank expression, swollen abdomen. Examination of their feces revealed that they were heavily infected with hookworms. Shortly before these photographs were taken, two of their siblings had died. Fourteen months after being treated for their infection, the boys looked completely different (bottom photographs).

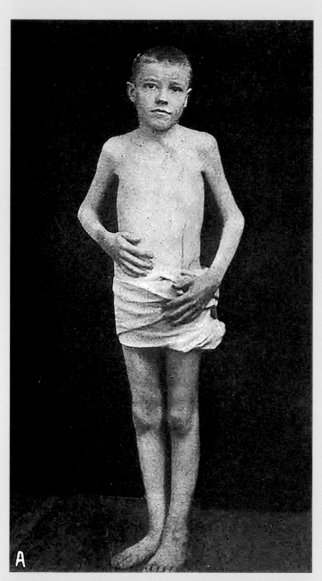

Bryan Shell, from Arkansas, was thirteen, anemic, undeveloped physically for his age, and extremely thin. Tests showed that he was infected with hookworms.

It took nine thymol treatments, each a week apart, to rid his body of the parasites. At the end of his treatment, Bryan posed for photograph B.

CHAPTER EIGHT

THE PRIVY PROBLEM

"Thymol in one hand and the gospel of health in the other."
—W. S. Rankin, **North Carolina secretary of health**

CHARLES STILES HAD HIS DOUBTS ABOUT ERADICATING the American Murderer within five years. Maybe the RSC could examine and treat tens of thousands of infected people in every southern state. But Stiles had visited dispensaries and talked to families, and he suspected that half of those given hookworm medicine never took it. Thymol could be dangerous when it wasn't used as directed. A few well-publicized deaths scared people away, even though the fatalities had been the result of improper use.

He told Rose, "I do not mean to discourage the clinics for they are doing good advertising, but I am more and more convinced as time goes on that their curative value is overrated."

As Stiles saw it, all the thymol in the world would do little good if the hookworm epidemic wasn't stopped where it started. In the outhouse.

Children learn about hookworms from two doctors at an Alabama dispensary. The man sitting at the table was the sanitary inspector. The other was a local doctor who volunteered to assist at the dispensary. Young people liked to look through the microscope at hookworms.

THE IDEAL PRIVY

The best way to prevent infection from intestinal parasites and diseases was an indoor toilet connected to a sewer system. But in the early twentieth century, only cities and some larger towns had built them. Millions of southerners—about 80 percent of the population—lived in rural areas without sewers.

During 1910–1914, Stiles and the RSC fieldworkers conducted a large survey of a quarter million rural homes in 653 southern counties. Half the houses had no privy, and residents defecated on open ground. About 45 percent of homes had a primitive privy, in which waste dropped on the ground surface underneath a seat and was exposed to animals, flies, and

County health departments printed flyers like this to urge residents to build and maintain effective sanitary privies as a way to prevent diseases.

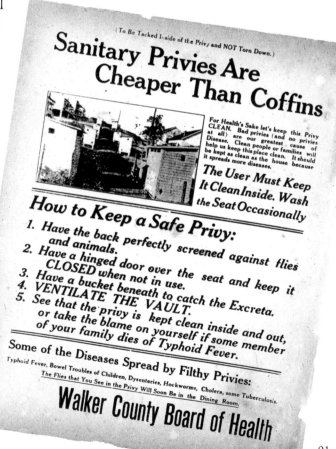

(To Be Tacked Inside of the Privy and NOT Torn Down.)

Sanitary Privies Are Cheaper Than Coffins

For Health's Sake let's keep this Privy CLEAN. Bad privies (and no privies at all) are our greatest cause of Disease. Clean people or families will help us keep this place clean. It should be kept as clean as the house because it spreads more diseases.

The User Must Keep It Clean Inside. Wash the Seat Occasionally

How to Keep a Safe Privy:

1. Have the back perfectly screened against flies and animals.
2. Have a hinged door over the seat and keep it CLOSED when not in use.
3. Have a bucket beneath to catch the Excreta.
4. VENTILATE THE VAULT.
5. See that the privy is kept clean inside and out, or take the blame on yourself if some member of your family dies of Typhoid Fever.

Some of the Diseases Spread by Filthy Privies:

Typhoid Fever, Bowel Troubles of Children, Dysenteries, Hookworms, Cholera, some Tuberculosis.
The Flies that You See in the Privy Will Soon Be in the Dining Room.

Walker County Board of Health

water runoff. Less than 1 percent (about 2,200 homes) had a privy that Stiles considered even minimally effective.

He was afraid it would take at least a generation to get all these people to change their sanitary habits. Meanwhile, Stiles did his best to educate them. At every opportunity, he hammered home the message that soil pollution was a great danger to the public, particularly children. "All fresh human feces," he said, "should be accepted as dangerous and should be treated as if they were actually a virulent poison."

When there was no municipal sewer system available, Stiles advised the homeowner to connect his toilet to a septic tank—a large cement, watertight container that collected wastewater. Septic tanks were expensive to install, and Stiles knew that few rural southerners could afford one. An outhouse was the best he could hope for.

At the PHS Marine Hospital in Wilmington, North Carolina, Stiles worked with L. L. Lumsden and Norman Roberts to design a safe and effective sanitary privy for areas without sewer systems. They called it the LRS privy (based on their initials).

Feces and urine landed under the privy floor in a watertight barrel where it decomposed and liquefied. After the level of the water in the barrel got too high, the excess flowed into a smaller tank. When that tank filled up, the liquid had to be emptied.

The PHS scientists recommended boiling it in order to kill bacteria and hookworm eggs. Then the liquid could be used as fertilizer on gardens and

Three PHS officers—Lumsden, Roberts, and Stiles—developed the LRS sanitary privy for use in rural areas. It was expensive and complicated to build, making it impractical for poor southern farmers.

fields. A less safe disposal method was burying unboiled liquid at least 2 feet deep (60 cm), downhill from water sources.

The LRS privy reduced odor. An oil film on the water stopped mosquitoes from breeding in the privy, and screens over openings prevented flies from carrying intestinal bacteria on their legs to the family's food.

A few communities required their residents to use an LRS privy. But it was too costly and complicated for most people to build and use.

The Rockefeller Sanitary Commission took a more realistic approach, recommending a pit privy instead. The outhouse was placed over a pit several feet deep and located away from a water source. When the pit was almost filled with waste, the homeowner had to dig a new pit, move the outhouse over it, and fill in the old pit with dirt.

Stiles insisted that only the LRS privy would do, arguing it was worth the cost to avoid any chance of disease. The RSC was willing to compromise in order to get more people to use a sanitary outhouse. A Commission report said, "Probably the pit privy represents the highest type of sanitation that some localities will be able to develop for years to come." Stiles remained critical of the decision.

As a result of encouragement from the state health boards and the hookworm dispensaries, thousands of people eventually built new sanitary privies. But this part of the RSC program was not a great success. People didn't like the unpleasant task of cleaning an outhouse. Many poor rural southerners had neither the time nor money to build even a pit privy. Tenant farmers and sharecroppers didn't own the land or

Health department officials and sanitary inspectors took their hookworm demonstrations to county and state fairs, where they could reach thousands of visitors. Kentucky's state health director (in bowtie and shirtsleeves) demonstrates how a cement septic tank is built. Stiles and the PHS recommended an underground septic tank as a safer way to deal with human waste than the typical privy. Twelve thousand people viewed this model, but most farmers couldn't afford one.

Schools became important partners in the hookworm eradication campaign. The study of hookworm disease was added to the curriculum in most southern states. The RSC acknowledged the role of teachers, calling them "the most effective allies the field directors have found."

Examinations revealed that every child in this Mississippi school (top) was infected. When the photograph was taken, the majority of them had been treated. Children in this Tennessee school group (bottom) received treatment for hookworm disease.

houses where they lived, and landowners weren't always willing to pay for their tenants' outhouses.

REACHING THE CHILDREN

The RSC understood that children suffered the most from hookworm disease. To reach them, the RSC took its campaign into the schools. Wickliffe Rose had spent his career involved in education and was personally acquainted with many of the South's educational leaders. He persuaded them to cooperate with the RSC project.

Many rural schools were open just four months of the year, October to February, so that children could work with their parents during the growing season. With the consent of school superintendents, the sanitary inspectors contacted teachers during the school term and asked to survey classes for hookworm infection.

Not only would this identify infected children, but it also provided a hint at hookworm rates in the community. Southern schools were segregated by race, and the inspectors visited both White and Black schools.

Teachers had already noticed the learning difficulties and low attendance of certain students. If hookworm treatment could solve those problems, the teachers were eager to help.

The sanitary inspectors supplied them with bottles to send home with students. Parents were told to gather a small amount of stool sample from a child and return it in the bottle. All children in a school were examined in the same way, and no one was singled out.

When the bottles came back, the teachers passed the samples to the state's health laboratory to be checked for hookworm eggs. The lab sent the results to parents by private letter to avoid stigmatizing a child or the family. The sanitary inspectors treated infected children at no charge.

In eleven southern states, about 549,000 rural schoolchildren from age six to eighteen were tested. Nearly four in ten (39 percent) were infected with hookworms. Teachers often were, too. In some counties, the rate of infection was much higher.

The number of actual infections across the South might have been even greater.

Not all children attended school, including those who were sick and weak with hookworm disease. The survey missed them.

Teachers saw improvement among the children who received thymol treatment. One Georgia educator wrote to a sanitary inspector about the noticeable change in his students' work: "They are cheerful and studious, now, where before they were peevish and stupid."

HOOKWORM LESSONS

As scientific secretary for the RSC, Stiles produced informational pamphlets aimed at teachers, students, and their parents. He didn't shy away from a topic usually avoided in public or in a mixed class of boys and girls—human excrement. In the introduction to one pamphlet, he wrote, *"Human life is at stake, and in preparing this circular we must state facts in plain English."*

In another, Stiles—the son of a minister—cited scripture verses to remind devout churchgoers that the Bible warned against soil pollution. His advice to use a sanitary privy, including the Bible reference, reappeared in newspaper articles throughout the South.

In the first year of the RSC program, sanitary inspectors passed out more than half a million hookworm pamphlets to schools. Teachers used the information supplied by the RSC and their state to craft lessons about hookworm and sanitation.

Most children had experienced ground itch. For the first time, they learned that it was the result of hookworm larvae burrowing into their skin. The students found out how the parasite settled in the small intestine and sucked their blood. They learned how to prevent infection by using sanitary privies and wearing shoes.

A few teachers were initially too modest to discuss the intimate details of hookworm disease. Stiles urged them to overcome their qualms, and most did. "You will save human life," he said, "just as surely as does the man who plunges into a stream to rescue a drowning child."

In some cases, sanitary inspectors and local doctors visited country schools to talk about hookworms. One of the inspectors designed his program "to make the story so simple, so direct, so vivid that every child will feel it tingle on the bottom of his bare foot when he walks on polluted soil."

A Mississippi teacher (center) poses among her students at the site of a hookworm dispensary. She arranged for every student and parent to attend a lecture about hookworm and to get examined. The teacher attended the same school when she was a child, and the families knew and trusted her.

Officials in Varnado, Louisiana, thanked the sanitary inspector for coming to their school, in which 85 percent of the students were infected. In a letter, they told of the enormous improvement in class performance, attention, and energy after the children were cured. "In short, we have here in our school-rooms today about 120 bright, rosy-faced children, whereas had you not been sent here to treat them we would have had that many pale-faced, stupid children."

The RSC also considered schools to be centers of a rural community. By maintaining clean and well-built privies and insisting that students use them, a school became a model of proper sanitation for children and families that didn't have an outhouse.

The Commission persuaded states and communities to upgrade their school facilities. In 1912, not a single country schoolhouse in Alabama had a privy, putting 350,000 children at risk of hookworm infection. Later that year, the state announced that it would fund a new school building only if the plans included two sanitary

Many community groups joined the hookworm campaign. They provided education about the parasite, promoted sanitary homes, and encouraged residents to be examined and treated. These women belonged to the Civil League of Colored Women, in Salisbury, North Carolina.

privies. North Carolina had a similar regulation. Louisiana and Virginia also required privies in every public school.

THE COMMUNITY STEPS UP

As the RSC work continued, local residents volunteered to help in the hookworm effort.

Women's groups raised money for thymol treatments and organized sanitation committees to improve the health of their communities. In Arkansas, the Federation of Women's Clubs established a hookworm committee to ramp up interest in sanitation. The group pushed for school inspections and improved privies, and it arranged lectures to educate children and the public about good hygiene. In North Carolina, the Woman's Betterment Association of Wake (County) funded the distribution of hookworm medicine.

Individuals lent a hand, too. In Mississippi, a woman collected containers from the sanitary inspector at her county's dispensary. She distributed them to her friends, urging them to send back a sample of their feces to be examined. After the ones diagnosed with a hookworm infection had taken their medicine, gained weight, and felt better, other neighbors asked to be tested, too. Thanks to one woman, a hundred people received treatment.

A Kentucky woman walked with her family several miles to be examined at a dispensary. The next day she returned to get a box of containers to hand out to her neighbors, some of whom had been too embarrassed to go to the dispensary themselves. Eventually, she brought back 146 stool samples to the dispensary. After the samples were checked, the woman collected the medicine and delivered it to each infected person. Because she couldn't read, she took along a young boy to read the instructions to her neighbors.

Still, Charles Stiles had been right. Not everyone would take the thymol treatment, either out of mistrust or fear. One mother learned that hookworm was the reason her severely infected children had been sick for several years, but she refused to let them be treated.

A Georgian wrote to his local newspaper and criticized those who wouldn't cooperate with the state's hookworm program. "Surely it is time that children should receive at least as much attention as the hogs and cows," he said. "Mothers and fathers who are too ignorant or indifferent to have their children given proper treatment should be forced to do so for the benefit of generations yet unborn."

This woman, posing with a pipe in her mouth, convinced her reluctant Kentucky neighbors to be examined at a dispensary.

Kentucky teacher, Mr. B., brought stool samples from his students to a dispensary. Everyone, including him, was infected. Teachers were important in the hookworm campaign, educating families and urging them to build sanitary privies.

Tennessee teacher Mary Pollard volunteered to assist with record-keeping at her local county dispensary.

SATISFIED CUSTOMERS

Despite failing to convince all southerners to be examined and treated, the Commission and the state boards of health heard many uplifting stories. Doctors sent letters about hookworm happy endings to the RSC or their state health director.

One physician described James, a Mississippi boy who had once been bright and energetic. Gradually, he became exhausted by his short walk to school, fell behind in his schoolwork, and stopped playing with his friends. By the time the doctor examined James, the boy had developed pica and was severely anemic. His feces were full of hookworm eggs. After two or three thymol treatments, James regained his strength and energy.

A North Carolina doctor wrote, "I wish you could see the many bright, healthy children that a year or so ago were without health and with no hope for the future. Words cannot tell the great good that has been accomplished."

Patients sent letters of appreciation, too. In December 1912, Joe McFarland wrote to the state director of Kentucky's hookworm commission, explaining that he had always been weak and pale. When he attended the dispensary in his town about five months before, his examination showed that he was heavily infected with hookworms. He was such a serious case that the field doctor sent him to the PHS Marine Hospital in Wilmington, North Carolina, where Charles Stiles was stationed.

Joe reported that he underwent twenty-five days of treatment at the hospital, during which he expelled 2,464 hookworms. His weight jumped 40 pounds (18 kg). "I am now mining coal and can do as much work as any man," Joe wrote, "and I never feel tired. . . . I will never cease to be grateful."

Even government leaders praised the hookworm campaign. In 1913, U.S. Senator James Vardaman of Mississippi wrote his state's health director, "If I had been told some years ago that hookworm was so prevalent in Mississippi, I could not have believed it. The disease has done a great deal of damage, and those engaged in exterminating it deserve the gratitude of all men."

Significant progress had been made since the beginning of the hookworm campaign when less than a fifth of the South's physicians examined or treated patients for the parasite. Yet Rose was disappointed that the RSC hadn't motivated more doctors. In a 1914 RSC report not made public, he wrote, "The [medical] profession as a whole is not doing all that one might expect in combatting the disease."

Stiles shared Rose's view that many doctors continued to ignore hookworm disease even though it was "so easy to recognize, so easy to treat." At a Virginia medical conference in November 1914, he announced, "The average Southern physician today is not interested in the subject [hookworm disease]. He does not make a diagnosis, and when he does make a diagnosis he does not treat the patient."

Other physicians at the conference strenuously disagreed and criticized Stiles, charging that he was not a medical doctor. After twelve years, Stiles still had not learned to be tactful when discussing hookworm.

CHAPTER NINE
A CURSE IS LIFTED

"Theoretically, hook-worm disease is one
of the easiest of all diseases to prevent. Practically the
undertaking is one of the most difficult."

—J. B. Elliott, Alabama physician

WHEN HE READ THE GLOWING REPORTS ABOUT THE
RSC's campaign, Frederick Gates began to plan a bigger undertaking.
Half of Earth's population lived in the zone around the equator, and
hundreds of millions of those people were infected with hookworms. It was time to
fight the parasite beyond the United States.

In 1913, Gates organized the launch of the Rockefeller Foundation, a philanthropy
with John D. Rockefeller Jr. as its president. Part of the Foundation was set up to
tackle hookworm using the RSC's approach. Known as the International Health
Commission (IHC), it was designed to assist governments in developing public
health programs.

As a start, the British government invited the Rockefeller Foundation and IHC to take the hookworm program into the British Empire's colonies and territories. Now the Foundation could help people in every part of the world—many millions more than the RSC had reached in the American South.

THE RSC ENDS

Meanwhile, the RSC continued its work in the U.S. Its original funding was intended for just five years, until December 31, 1914. By the summer of 1914, Gates believed the RSC had met its goals.

In a letter to John D. Rockefeller Sr., he wrote, "Hookworm disease has not only been recognized, bounded and limited, it has been reduced to one of the minor infections of the south."

That August, Rockefeller sent a letter to the RSC members, confirming the Commission's end and thanking them for their service. Among the RSC's achievements, he said, was showing southerners that hookworm disease was a danger and demonstrating how to fix the problem. "The chief purpose of the commission may thus be deemed to have been accomplished."

The news was an unpleasant surprise to everyone involved in the hookworm project, including most Commission board members. Although they knew about the five-year limit, they expected an extension past December 1914. There was much more to do in the South. But Gates and Rockefeller had decided that the RSC would stick to the original schedule.

Wickliffe Rose persuaded Gates to allow a few additional months for the RSC to finish projects in some of the states. Gates required any future work to be done through the Rockefeller Foundation's International Health Commission, and Rose was appointed its director. The IHC hired only a handful of the RSC's doctors who had been working as sanitary inspectors.

Gates and Rose didn't ask Charles Stiles to join the IHC. He had irritated them. Stiles spoke out against the RSC's recommendation of a pit privy over his preferred LRS design. He claimed the dispensaries' treatment success was exaggerated. And he was publicly critical when Gates ended the RSC.

The International Health Division

In 1913, the Rockefellers established the Rockefeller Foundation with a division devoted to public health. The International Health Commission (IHC) took over the work of the Rockefeller Sanitary Commission, fighting hookworm both in the United States and around the world. The name changed to International Health Board (IHB) in 1916 and to International Health Division (IHD) in 1927.

After the RSC campaign ended in 1914, the IHC continued hookworm education, treatment, and prevention in the South, but with state governments taking on more responsibility. By the end of the 1920s, the hookworm program had wound down, and states operated health departments with full-time staff in many counties. This had been one of Rockefeller and Gates's original aims.

The International Health Division's public health efforts throughout the world went on for nearly four decades. Its doctors and staff worked in dozens of countries. Besides hookworm, they focused on tuberculosis, malaria, and yellow fever.

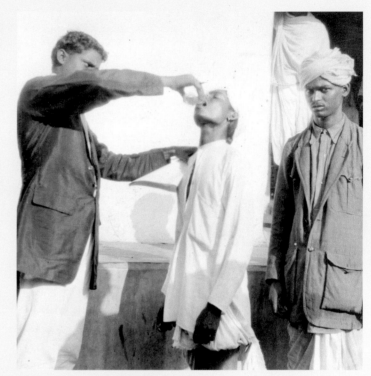

A boy in India receives treatment for hookworm.

In 1920, IHB doctors treated this nine-year-old Brazilian boy for worms. He holds a board displaying some of the parasites expelled from his intestine.

Until his retirement in 1930, Charles Stiles worked as head of the Hygienic Laboratory's Zoology Division, specializing in parasites. He died from a heart ailment in January 1941 at age seventy-three.

Throughout his five years as the RSC's scientific secretary, Stiles had also worked as head of the Hygienic Laboratory's Zoology Division. After the Commission dissolved, he continued in that PHS position.

MISSION ACCOMPLISHED

At the end of 1914, the RSC formally reviewed the previous five years. The Commission had involved the majority of counties in eleven states in running almost 600 dispensaries. Working with local physicians and state laboratories, it had microscopically examined nearly 1.3 million people. Overall, at least a third of them were infected with hookworms and received thymol. Among examined children, about 40 percent carried the parasite. In some states, these infection rates were higher.

Before the hookworm campaign began, Stiles guessed that about 2 million southerners were infected. But after five years, he concluded that the number was at least 3 million. The RSC hadn't come close to identifying and curing them all. Despite handing out medicine to hundreds of thousands of people, no one at the RSC was sure how many had actually taken the thymol.

The Commission estimated that it educated 20 million southerners about hookworm disease. It helped physicians and state health officials to recognize the parasite as a serious health problem and to reduce hookworm's threat through improved sanitation, testing, and treatment.

By strengthening southern public health agencies, the RSC enabled them to fight not only hookworm, but also epidemic diseases such as tuberculosis, typhoid fever, malaria, and pellagra.

Admirers believed that Stiles and the RSC saved the South. They had proved that the stereotype of the backward southerner was unfair and inaccurate. One Chicago newspaper columnist wrote in spring 1914: "All the peoples we call indolent and lazy have hook-worm. They have not been equal to northern people in energy and power in the past; but they will be. . . . Watch the south develop."

The Rockefeller Sanitary Commission's hookworm campaign spurred counties to develop public health programs, especially in rural areas. During the Depression, the federal government funded additional health outreach. This visiting nurse brings hookworm medicine to a rural family in Alabama in 1939.

Around 1916, the International Health Board created a booklet, *The Story of a Boy Who Did Not Grow Up to Be a Tall Strong Man*, to teach children and families about hookworm infections. These images are from the version published in 1920.

The boy, Tom Hardy, walks through outhouse seepage where tiny red hookworms lurk. He develops ground itch when the hookworm larvae attack his feet. As the story continues, Tom goes to a dispensary, receives medicine, and is cured of his hookworm infection.

HOOKWORM ERADICATED?

Over the next dozen years, the International Health Commission worked with southern state governments to continue efforts against hookworm infections. In 1927, the Rockefeller Foundation announced, "Hookworm disease has almost disappeared from the United States." The news was widely reported in the press.

Charles Stiles disagreed.

After his 1930 retirement from the Public Health Service, Stiles drove thousands of miles through the Gulf-Atlantic states. He was on the lookout for hookworm infections.

Stiles published the results of his trips in respected scientific journals. Comparing his observations to those of similar travels from

The RSC's surveys of rural school sanitation motivated states to establish stricter rules about privy construction. Progress was slow, however. In this 1921 photograph (left), the privies behind a West Virginia schoolhouse are open at the bottom, are built on a hill, and are too close together. Animals can gain access to human waste and spread it on their feet. Rainwater flowing down the hill carries waste toward the adjacent schoolhouse. Inside the school (below), children do their lessons. Several are barefoot, putting them at risk of hookworm infection when they visit the privy.

A photograph taken at a nearby school shows a primitive, unsanitary privy.

1902 to 1910, he acknowledged that he had seen lighter hookworm infections and fewer dirt-eaters. But he made clear that hookworm disease had definitely not disappeared as many thought.

He quoted the results of microscopic examinations of 121,000 people performed in 1929 at state laboratories in nine southern states. About 28 percent of the patients were infected. In his own survey of 18,000 schoolchildren, Stiles visually diagnosed at least a quarter of them with hookworm disease symptoms.

This convinced him that parents and schools were overlooking cases because they had been incorrectly told that the disease was eradicated. Stiles wrote to John D. Rockefeller Jr. and the Rockefeller Foundation, asking them to retract their claim. No one replied.

Many southern farmers disregarded the warnings that hookworms entered the body through skin. These photographs from the 1930s show that the barefoot habit was slow to disappear. Some families couldn't afford shoes for their children. Other people found it more comfortable to go barefoot.

The North Carolina girl, age thirteen, is planting sweet potatoes (top left). The young son of a South Carolina sharecropper takes a break from his chores (top right). An Alabama tenant farmer and his family work in a cotton field. Only the father wears shoes (bottom).

Even though the RSC failed to wipe out hookworm, Stiles admitted in late 1931 that "the public health advancement of the South since 1901 has been absolutely marvelous."

A 1940 comparison of hookworm infection rates in six southern states showed the progress. The average rate of infection among residents of those states dropped from about 37 percent during the 1910–1914 period to 11 percent during 1930–1938. Three-quarters of the 1930s cases were light infections that caused no symptoms. The majority of infections occurred among children ages five to nineteen.

The American Murderer had not been eradicated, but the parasite was no longer the widespread threat it had once been. The burden of severe hookworm disease on millions of southerners was lifted, ending a medical fiasco that had cursed the South for generations.

Even after years of public health campaigns, hookworm didn't disappear from the South. These Texas children, photographed in 1939, are infected with the parasite.

CHAPTER TEN

THE BLOODSUCKER LIVES ON

"If the soil were not befouled with human excrement, there would be no hookworm infection."

—Wickliffe Rose

B Y THE END OF WORLD WAR II IN 1945, PUBLIC HEALTH officials hoped that they were at last on the way to ridding the South of hookworm disease.

The southeastern states had become more urbanized. Fewer southerners lived on small farms. As the South's economy improved, people found jobs at higher pay. They had access to more nutritious food and ate a healthier diet. Even if someone became infected with hookworms, his or her well-nourished body could better withstand the blood loss caused by the parasites.

Despite the work of the Rockefeller Sanitary Commission, sanitation in U.S. homes continued to be a problem for decades. Human excrement piles up under this crude privy in Maryland in the early 1940s.

Towns and cities installed water and sewer systems to keep drinking water clean and to safely dispose of human waste. In rural areas, county health departments supervised sewage disposal. During the 1930s, the federal government had funded construction of hundreds of thousands of privies throughout the South. These sanitation changes greatly reduced the spread of intestinal parasites and diseases.

STILL HIDING IN AMERICA

In the 1950s and 1960s, examinations of stool samples by state laboratories in Texas, South Carolina, Georgia, and Kentucky showed that rates of hookworm infection had dropped from earlier decades. Yet the American Murderer persisted.

One study during the 1950s turned up infection rates as high as 60 percent in some rural Alabama counties. In the early 1970s, a survey indicated that 12 percent of children living on the rural coast of Georgia were infected. Around the same time, 15 percent of elementary students in rural Kentucky carried the parasite. A 1987 survey of Central American migrant farmworkers in North Carolina revealed that half of them were infected with hookworms.

American public health authorities have not recently conducted large-scale hookworm surveys. But there are signs that *Necator americanus* still infects some southerners, especially those who live in rural poverty. Fortunately, few infections are severe enough to damage health.

In a limited study of one Alabama county, published in 2017, about a third of the examined people harbored low numbers of *Necator* worms. Despite having indoor toilets, they lived in homes with faulty waste disposal.

To have proper sanitation, a rural household needs its own septic system to deal with each toilet flush. The waste follows a pipe from the toilet to an underground tank on the property. Heavy solid material settles to the bottom of the tank and decomposes. The liquid slowly drains from the tank and percolates through a specially designed system in the soil that filters and cleans it before it trickles into the groundwater.

For a septic system to work effectively, the remaining solids in the tank must be periodically pumped out and safely disposed of at a waste treatment plant. If the septic system fails, the waste bubbles to the soil surface or backs up into the house.

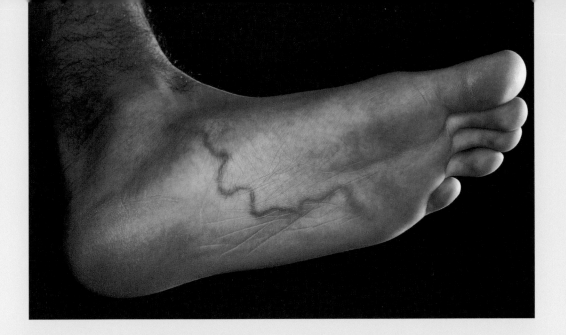

Danger on the Beach

Today's beachgoers in the tropics or subtropics, including the southeastern United States, sometimes take home an unintended guest. Hookworm species that infect dogs may enter a human's body if bare skin comes in contact with animal feces. Warm, sandy beaches where dogs run loose are perfect spots for these hookworm eggs and larvae to survive.

Cats also transmit a species of hookworm that penetrates human skin. Children playing in sandboxes might be infected if cats or dogs have defecated in the sand.

In a nonhuman host, these animal hookworms develop and infect their host's small intestine just as *Necator* and *Ancylostoma* hookworms do in humans. But a dog or cat hookworm larva isn't adapted to migrate from the human skin and travel deeper into the body. Instead, it tunnels through the skin layer for weeks, leaving an intensely itchy rash behind as it moves.

The rash, called creeping eruption, looks like raised, squiggly red lines. Doctors prescribe medicines to relieve the itch and kill the burrowing larva.

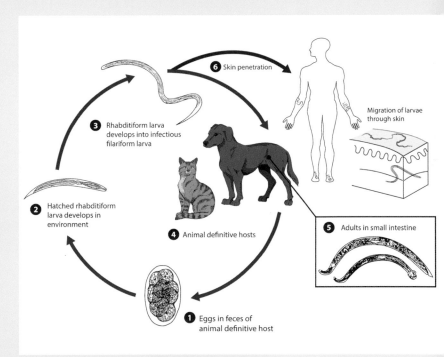

This diagram summarizes the life cycle of a dog or cat hookworm. When the larva invades a human, it stays in the skin layer and causes creeping eruption (shown in this man's foot). To avoid being infected at beaches in the tropics and subtropics, wear shoes and sit on a mat to avoid skin contact with the sand.

Home septic systems are expensive to install, and the cost of regular maintenance can strain a family's budget. State and county health regulations usually require a system when a house isn't connected to a sewer, though enforcement varies. Untreated human waste is too often flushed away from a house through pipes and ditches directly into lawns, woods, or fields.

The recent Alabama study hints at the consequences of inadequate sanitation. In the United States, about a fifth of houses aren't connected to a city or town sewer system. If waste removal is flawed and temperatures and soil conditions are right, hookworm eggs and larvae can thrive. People may be infected when they walk or play in sewage-contaminated ground. Human waste also endangers the community by flowing into streams and rivers and spreading intestinal diseases into the drinking water.

THE DANGEROUS TRIO

Although the number of hookworm infections in America is probably low, the parasite is a significant threat to health in other parts of the world. Experts estimate that hookworms infect 500 million to 1 billion people on every continent except Antarctica.

Children play in Kenya. Their bare feet put them at risk of a hookworm infection.

Countries in the subtropics and tropics have ideal environments for a hookworm's survival. The most infections occur in sub-Saharan Africa, southeastern Asia, China, and South America. Hookworms spread in places lacking good sanitation, such as poor rural areas and urban slums. People have higher rates of infection along the coasts where moist, sandy soil is perfect for a larva.

Worldwide, *Necator americanus* is the most common human hookworm. *Ancylostoma duodenale*, which is more dangerous because each worm sucks more blood, accounts for less than 15 percent of human hookworm infections.

Hookworm isn't the only parasite that threatens people in these regions. It is one of a trio of intestinal worms spread from person to person through soil contaminated with feces. Known as soil-transmitted helminths (STH), the group also includes *Ascaris lumbricoides* (a human roundworm commonly called *Ascaris*) and *Trichuris trichiura* (human whipworm).

In some parts of the world, farmers fertilize their fields with human feces. When farmworkers walk barefoot, they risk becoming infected with hookworm larvae through their skin. Produce grown in the fields could be contaminated with *Ancylostoma duodenale.* If the food is swallowed without being washed or cooked, the hookworm will infect the diner. These men live in India (top) and Cambodia (bottom), two countries where hookworm cases occur today.

Without extensive surveys, health experts have to guess at infection numbers. They estimate that at least 1.5 billion people carry one or more of these parasites. *Ascaris* infects about 800 million to 1.2 billion, and whipworm from 600 million to 1 billion people. Though not common in the U.S., both *Ascaris* and whipworm infections do occur, usually in the southern states.

Unlike hookworm whose larvae invade through skin, *Ascaris* and whipworm infect a person who swallows the microscopic eggs. Perhaps she ate fruit and vegetables fertilized by human feces in the field, without first rinsing, peeling, or cooking. Or after touching contaminated dirt, he put his hands in his mouth or ate without washing them first.

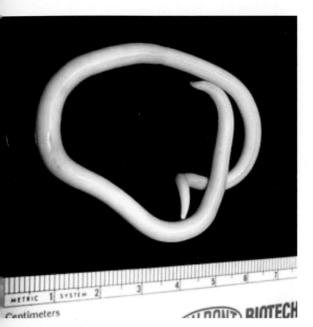

An adult female *Ascaris lumbricoides* worm. Females are larger than males and can grow to more than 12 inches (30 cm).

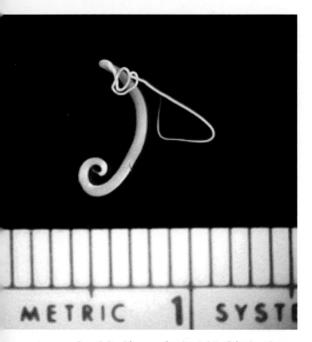

An adult whipworm is about 1 to 2 inches long (3 to 5 cm). Its name comes from its appearance: a thin, threadlike front end and a thicker rear end like a whip handle.

The swallowed *Ascaris* eggs land in the small intestine, where they hatch. The larvae penetrate the intestine wall and travel through the circulatory system. Like hookworm larvae, they are eventually carried to the lungs, move up the windpipe and are swallowed. Back in the small intestine again, they mature and mate.

Adults can be more than 1 foot long (30 cm), and females, which are larger than males, are often as thick as a pencil. *Ascaris* don't suck blood. Instead, they eat food ingested by their human host. Females produce as many as 200,000 eggs a day, which leave the host's body in feces.

People who carry only a few *Ascaris* worms tend to have no symptoms. But an infection with many worms can cause a cough, shortness of breath, abdominal pain, vomiting, and diarrhea. The worms may become so plentiful that they block part of the intestine. In children, an *Ascaris* infection affects appetite and the body's ability to absorb nutrients from food, causing malnutrition. The child's growth and development suffer.

Human whipworm eggs hatch in the small intestine after being ingested. As a larva develops, it moves to the large intestine where it spends its life. Adult whipworms are about 1 to 2 inches long (3 to 5 cm), with females larger than males. The whipworm's head attaches to the intestine wall, from which it gets its nutrients. Unlike hookworms, it doesn't suck blood. Female worms produce about 3,000 to 10,000 eggs a day, which leave the host in feces.

While a light whipworm infection usually causes no symptoms, a heavy infection can create abdominal pain, diarrhea, weakness, anemia, and weight loss. Children carrying more than 200 worms may have dysentery and anemia and fail to grow normally.

A technician at the CDC (Centers for Disease Control and Prevention) holds a handful of *Ascaris* worms that passed from a child's small intestine in Kenya. Some people are hosts to hundreds of worms.

FIGHTING THE PARASITES

Most people don't die directly from an STH infection. But if they're heavily infected with one of this trio of intestinal worms, their bodies become susceptible to other diseases that might kill them. Pregnant women are at higher risk of miscarriage or death.

A country suffers economically when large numbers of its people can't work because parasite infections make them tired or sick. The nation's progress is in jeopardy if its children fail to grow physically and intellectually.

The Rockefeller Sanitary Commission aimed to improve the lives of southerners by helping them achieve better health. More than a century later, international public health programs have a similar mission.

A community volunteer in the West African country of Côte d'Ivoire (Ivory Coast) gives antiparasite medicine to children.

In countries where STHs are common, these groups regularly treat people for worms. Thymol, used by the RSC, has been replaced with new, safe, and effective medicines. The same oral drug kills hookworm, *Ascaris,* and whipworm. The treatment typically focuses on preschool and school-age children. The regular deworming of hundreds of millions of children has brought down overall infections from *Ascaris* and whipworm, which are found more often in children than in adults.

Treatments have been less successful in controlling hookworm. Despite programs that emphasize proper sanitation and shoe-wearing, the worldwide hookworm infection rate hasn't dropped as much as health workers hoped. Drugs don't provide lasting protection. People are reinfected again and again because of poor sanitation or the practice of fertilizing crops with human excrement.

Some researchers worry that hookworms are becoming resistant to the medicines used to kill them. Others think that adults are more frequently exposed to hookworms, primarily through farming in feces-fertilized fields. To control the parasite, these scientists suggest treating entire communities, not just the children.

Many health experts believe that a vaccine is the best protection from hookworm's ravages. Current vaccine development targets *Necator americanus*, the most common species. If a vaccine can stimulate the body to fight off the majority of invading hookworms, people will have only mild infections. They will be less likely to experience the serious anemia and protein deficiencies that damage overall health.

Today, about 2.4 billion people worldwide don't use or have access to a sanitation method that stops human waste from polluting their environment. Pit latrines and septic tanks are often improperly built and maintained, allowing waste to leak. Hundreds of millions of people defecate and urinate on the ground or in water sources such as rivers and lakes. This allows the spread of intestinal parasites and life-threatening bacterial diseases such as typhoid fever, dysentery, and cholera.

International organizations are working to develop effective and inexpensive toilets for

A technician in Tanzania uses a microscope to check a stool sample for STH infection.

places that lack sewer systems, electricity, or water. Gradual progress over several decades has improved conditions in some areas, but more remains to be done.

———

Hookworms evolved over thousands of years to become a successful human parasite. We have fought them by learning how they enter our bodies and how they reproduce. We have developed medicines to kill them and sanitation methods to stop their spread. These breakthroughs have improved the health of millions of people.

Yet after we think we've eliminated their threat, the parasites bounce back. The battle to protect ourselves from hookworm disease continues.

In many parts of the world, the worms are winning.

TIMELINE

1902

May
Stiles announces discovery of a second human hookworm, *Necator americanus.*

1838

Italian doctor Angelo Dubini discovers *Ancylostoma duodenale*, a human hookworm.

1854

German doctor Wilhelm Griesinger connects hookworm to severe anemia.

1899

U.S. Army doctor Bailey Ashford finds widespread hookworm disease in Puerto Rico.

1861–1865

American Civil War.

1898

Spanish-American War. German scientist Arthur Looss discovers how hookworms infect humans.

1867

Charles Stiles born in Spring Valley, New York.

1891

Stiles begins work at the USDA.

1890

Stiles receives a doctoral degree in zoology.

1880

Workers on the Gotthard Railway Tunnel, Switzerland, are infected with hookworms.

1886

Stiles travels to Europe to study.

August
Stiles becomes head of the Zoology Division of the PHS Hygienic Laboratory.

1902–1908
Stiles tours the South, raising awareness of hookworm disease.

1908
November
Stiles tells Walter Page about hookworm disease.

1909
October
John D. Rockefeller donates $1 million to eradicate hookworm disease in the South.

December
Wickliffe Rose becomes administrative secretary of the Rockefeller Sanitary Commission (RSC).

1913
Rockefeller Foundation established.

1941–1945
United States fights in World War II.

1941
Stiles dies of heart disease.

1930
Stiles retires from the PHS.

1915
International Health Commission takes over the hookworm campaign.

1914
December
RSC campaign in the South ends.

A sanitary inspector explains hookworm prevention at an Alabama dispensary.

GLOSSARY

alveoli: small air sacs in lungs where oxygen enters and carbon dioxide leaves the bloodstream.

Ancylostoma duodenale: a species of human hookworm sometimes called the Old World hookworm.

anemia: a medical condition in which a person lacks enough red blood cells to carry sufficient oxygen to the body's tissues. Symptoms include fatigue, weakness, pale skin.

Ascaris lumbricoides: a roundworm parasite found in humans.

autopsy: a surgical examination of a dead body to determine the cause of death.

cadaver: a dead human body.

capillary: tiny blood vessels connecting the smallest arteries and veins.

chlorosis: the historical name for iron-deficiency anemia.

cholera: an intestinal infection caused by a bacterium that is sometimes fatal. Symptoms include watery diarrhea and vomiting.

contagious disease: an illness spread by contact with a person who has the disease.

creeping eruption: the itchy, red, winding rash caused when dog or cat hookworm larvae infect human skin.

diarrhea: an intestinal ailment in which bowel movements are watery and frequent.

dissect: to cut open a dead body in order to study its internal parts.

dysentery: an intestinal disease with symptoms of abdominal pain, vomiting, and severe, often bloody diarrhea.

epidemic: a disease that spreads to many members of a population at the same time.

feces, or stool: solid body waste discharged from the intestines.

filariform: the hookworm larval stage that invades the human body.

ground itch: the itchy, red rash that develops where hookworm larvae penetrate the skin.

hookworm: a bloodsucking, parasitic worm that lives in the small intestine.

hookworm disease or **uncinariasis:** the illness caused by a hookworm infection. Symptoms include anemia, weakness, and abdominal pain.

infectious disease: an illness caused by an organism such as a bacterium, virus, or parasite that invades the body.

larva: the stage of a hookworm's development after hatching from an egg.

malaria: an infectious disease caused by parasitic microbes transmitted by mosquitoes. Symptoms include fever and chills. Occurs in wet areas where mosquitoes breed.

Necator americanus: a species of human hookworm, sometimes called the New World hookworm.

parasite: an animal or plant that benefits from living in, with, or on another organism and often harms its host.

pellagra: a disease caused by a diet lacking the vitamin niacin. Symptoms include skin rashes, diarrhea, mental disorders, and death.

pica: a constant craving for nonfood substances such as dirt, clay, and chalk. It can be a sign of iron deficiency.

pneumonia: a lung infection with symptoms of cough, chest pain, rapid breathing, fever.

privy, or **outhouse:** an outdoor toilet.

smallpox: a contagious, often fatal disease caused by a virus. Symptoms include high fever and skin sores.

STH, or **soil-transmitted helminths:** intestinal worms that spread through soil contaminated with feces.

tapeworm: a parasitic worm that lives in the intestines.

thymol: medicine swallowed to kill hookworms in the small intestine.

typhoid fever: an infectious disease caused by a bacterium that spreads through food and water contaminated with body waste. Symptoms include high fever, headache, reddish skin spots, and bleeding from intestines.

tuberculosis: a serious lung disease caused by a bacterium. Symptoms include cough, fever, chest pain, and weight loss.

vaccine: a special preparation of killed or weakened microbes that triggers the body to produce immunity to a disease.

villi: small, fingerlike structures lining the small intestine wall that absorb nutrients from digested food.

whipworm (Trichuris trichiura): a roundworm parasite found in humans.

yellow fever: a viral disease spread by mosquitoes. Symptoms include fever, vomiting, and body aches.

zoology: the study of animals.

This crowd attended a hookworm dispensary in Lattimore, North Carolina.

MORE TO EXPLORE

*Websites active at time of publication

Centers for Disease Control and Prevention
"Parasites—Hookworm"
cdc.gov/parasites/hookworm
Discover information about human hookworm, including symptoms of disease, prevention, and treatment.

Rockefeller Archive Center
The Rockefeller Foundation: A Digital History
rockfound.rockarch.org
Search "hookworm" to locate images and documents related to the Rockefeller Foundation's campaign against the parasite. Under the Health menu, find information, documents, and photographs about the Rockefeller Sanitary Commission and the International Health Division.

Unhooking the Hookworm
youtube.com/watch?v=OD-sDISDrKk
Check out a 1920 silent film about hookworm. Produced by the International Health Division for educational purposes, the film shows how the parasite infected a young boy. Watch a hookworm egg hatching, a larva entering a skin pore, and live adult larvae. See how a doctor examined a boy for infection.

Public Health Reports (1896–1970)
U.S. National Library of Medicine, National Institutes of Health
ncbi.nlm.nih.gov/pmc/journals/347/#pubhelathrepororig
Read Charles Stiles's reports about hookworm studies conducted at the U.S. Public Health Service. Scroll down to find the volume and pages listed in this book's bibliography.

Gross Science from *Nova*
"Hookworms and the Myth of the 'Lazy Southerner'"
youtube.com/watch?v=7BwgpYexMjk
Watch an illustrated summary of hookworm's effect on the American South.

PBS
The Rockefellers
pbs.org/wgbh/americanexperience/films/rockefellers
The website for this *American Experience* episode from 2000 contains information and photographs about John D. Rockefeller, his family, and their philanthropic work. Find articles about Frederick Gates and Ida Tarbell. Read excerpts from Tarbell's "The History of the Standard Oil Company." The transcript of the documentary is also available.

AUTHOR'S NOTE

American Murderer is the third book in my Medical Fiascoes series. Long before I explored the topics of the first two books (Civil War medicine in *Blood and Germs* and President Garfield's assassination in *Ambushed!*), I wrote about hookworms.

In a short book for young readers, I focused on the parasite's biology. I was fascinated by its ability to invade, hide in, and survive inside the human body. Later, while researching my books about American medicine in the early 1900s, I was surprised to discover that hookworms had an intriguing connection to that era. One name was associated with these parasites in the United States: Charles Wardell Stiles.

Stiles was among the scientists and physicians who dedicated their careers to public health. Their discoveries during the first part of the twentieth century solved medical mysteries, cured the sick, and prevented disease transmission.

Through his jobs at the U.S. Public Health Service and Department of Agriculture, Stiles had contact with subjects of my previous books: Surgeon General Walter Wyman, head of the PHS (*Red Madness, Bubonic Panic*); Dr. Joseph Goldberger, who solved the pellagra mystery (*Red Madness*); and Dr. Harvey Wiley, Father of the FDA (*The Poison Eaters*). As part of Stiles's efforts to improve sanitation in the South, he collaborated with PHS scientists working to end typhoid fever outbreaks (*Fatal Fever*). In recognition of Stiles's commitment to sanitary privies, Dr. Wiley gave him the German nickname Herr Geheimrath (Privy Councilor).

It took a worm scientist, not a medical doctor, to bring the hookworm problem to the country's attention. I located details about Charles Stiles's career and personal life in two short biographical pieces by Mark Sullivan and Frank G. Brooks, both based on information supplied by Stiles.

To find out what Stiles knew about hookworms before he identified *Necator americanus* in 1902, I reviewed scientists' papers from the 1800s. Stiles's own research reports revealed how he expanded that knowledge. To learn about recent advances in hookworm biology and treatments, I studied current books and articles by parasitologists and public health experts.

Next I investigated the Rockefeller Sanitary Commission's role in controlling America's hookworm epidemic. I read the Commission's *Annual Reports,* correspondence and memoirs by key participants, and newspaper and magazine articles from the period. Documents from the Rockefeller Archive Center were especially helpful. Stiles's 1939 article about the hookworm campaign provided his perspective. For additional insight, I consulted recent academic papers and books about the Rockefellers and the history of the RSC.

An account of hookworm disease in America is more than statistics. I searched for stories and images of victims, many of whom were children and teens. Photographs of farms, privies, dispensaries, doctors, and volunteers help to bring this history to life, and I've shared them with my readers.

In the course of my research, I came across two hookworm topics that recently received press coverage. I chose not to include these in the book's narrative because the information is speculative.

One discussed the idea that hookworm infections among southern Civil War soldiers severely weakened them and put them at a fighting disadvantage. After four years of unsanitary camp living, they took home their acquired infections when the war ended and further spread the parasite throughout the South. Northern soldiers contracted hookworms, too. But when they returned to their homes in cold climates, the parasite couldn't survive.

While this scenario is possible, it can't be verified. Hookworm disease hadn't been identified in the United States at the time of the Civil War, 1861–1865. Military surgeons knew nothing about it and, therefore, never diagnosed the ailment among soldiers.

The second topic involves the hypothesis that low levels of hookworm infection prevent allergies and autoimmune illnesses. According to this idea, the human immune system evolved alongside intestinal worms. When improved hygiene eliminated the worms from our bodies, the immune system was affected. The imbalance may result in serious allergic responses.

Some proponents have suggested that introducing hookworms into the intestine will cure these ailments. Most parasite scientists do not advocate this risky treatment. They don't believe sufficient evidence exists to prove the safety and effectiveness of a deliberate hookworm infection.

As I worked on *American Murderer* during the COVID-19 outbreak, I was conscious of the parallels between that pandemic and the hookworm epidemic in the South more than a century ago. In both cases, the human body faced a microscopic invader capable of causing serious illness and spreading to millions of people. Besides the physical effects, both diseases had a significant economic impact on individuals, families, and communities.

The challenges of controlling COVID-19 and hookworm were daunting. The responses to these public health crises in the United States—a century apart—illustrate the benefit of cooperation between private and government organizations in tackling a medical fiasco.

—*GJ*

ACKNOWLEDGMENTS

Thank you to all those who graciously shared their knowledge as they answered my questions and helped me find information and images for this book: The Rockefeller Archive Center's Barbara Shubinski, director of research and education; Renee Pappous, archivist; and Rachel Wimpee, assistant director of research and education. Joel Scogin, public health sanitarian, Department of Health, Tompkins County, New York. The staff of the Cornell University Library.

As always, I greatly appreciate the creativity and expertise of the team at Calkins Creek/ Astra Books for Young Readers, especially my talented and supportive editor, Carolyn P. Yoder. Thanks to them, my many months of research and writing have finally become a published book in the hands of readers.

—GJ

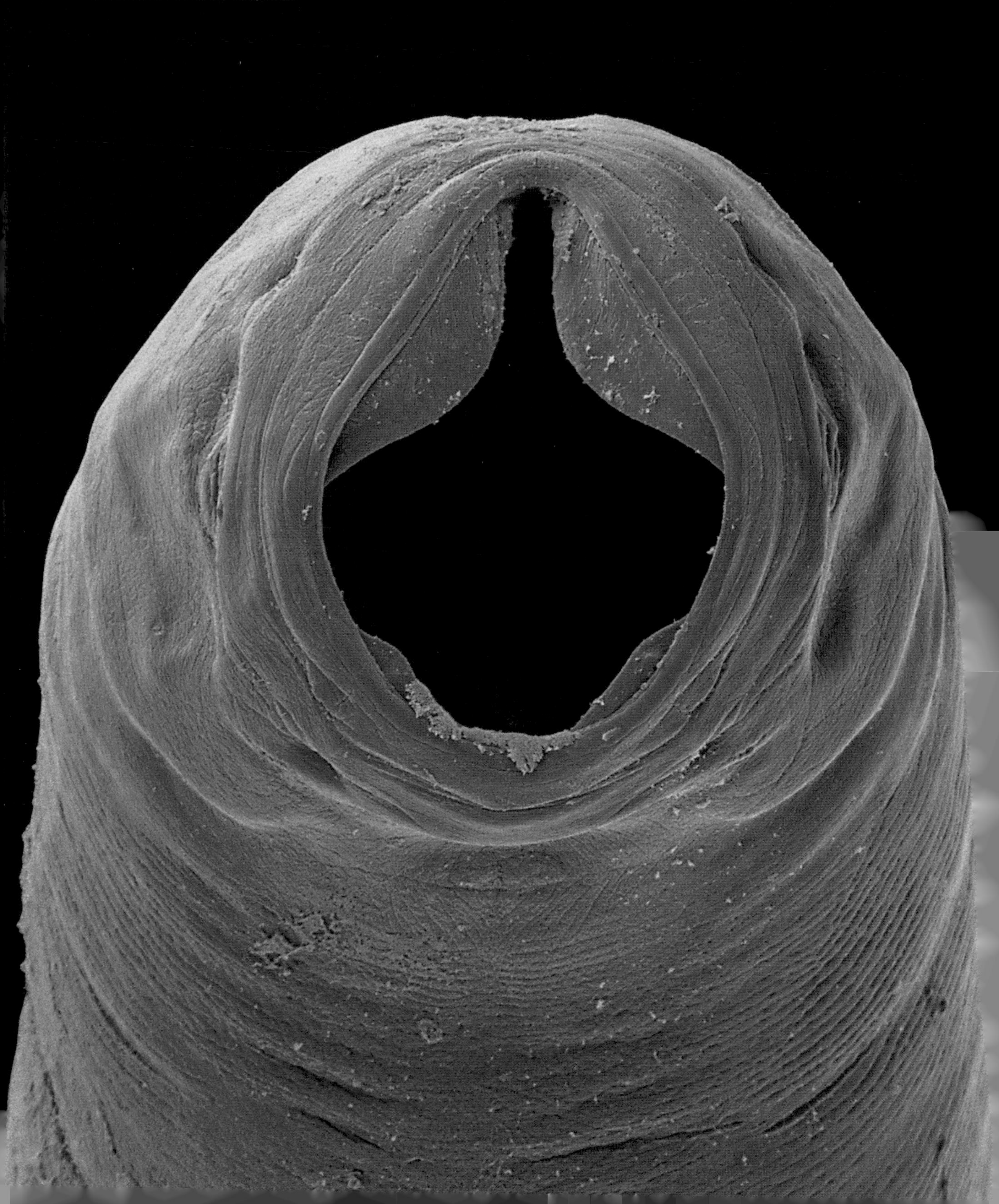

The head of *Necator americanus* magnified
1,650 times and color-enhanced

SOURCE NOTES

The source of each quotation in this book is found below. The citation indicates the first words of the quotation and its document source. The sources are listed either in the bibliography or below.

The following abbreviation is used:
RSC—Rockefeller Sanitary Commission for the Eradication of Hookworm Disease Annual Reports
RAC—Rockefeller Archive Center, Office of the Messrs. Rockefeller records

CHAPTER ONE
VAMPIRE (PAGE 8)
"The disease . . .": Stiles, "Hook-worm Disease in the South," p. 2434.
"What on earth . . .": Henry Wallace, quoted by Stiles in Sullivan, p. 320.
"If he represents . . .": same as above.

CHAPTER TWO
WORM SCIENTIST (PAGE 11)
"The little worm . . .": Bugnion, p. 382.

CHAPTER THREE
UNLOCKING SECRETS (PAGE 21)
"Nature goes along . . .": Arthur Looss, "Contribution to the Life Cycle of the Hookworm," 1898, in Kean, p. 309.
"This malady must surely . . .": Stiles, "Early History," 1939, p. 288.
"a disease, as easily recognized . . .": quoted in Stiles, "Early History," 1939, p. 289.
"If you find . . ." and "consider the possibility . . .": Stiles, "Early History," 1939, p. 289.
"in great numbers.": Ashford, "Ankylostomiasis in Puerto Rico," p. 553.
"In the new world . . ." and "although it is . . .": Stiles, "A New Species of Hookworm," p. 778.

CHAPTER FOUR
THE LAZINESS GERM (PAGE 34)

"Hookworm children are . . .": Stiles, "Hookworm Disease in Its Relation to the Negro," p. 1087.

"I returned to my hotel . . .": quoted in Bjorkman, p. 11609.

"is one of the most important . . .": Stiles, "Hook-worm Disease in the South," p. 2434.

"The disease in question . . .": same as above, p. 2433.

"at almost any place . . .": same as above, pp. 2433–34.

"'The Lazy Germ'": "Hunting Down the Lazy Germ," *Denver Republican*, quoted in *Washington Post*, October 25, 1903.

"that the 'germ of laziness' . . .": *New York Sun* reporter quoted in "Lazy Bug Joke Dead," *Washington Post*, October 30, 1909.

"'Yes; you might . . .'": Stiles quoted in same as above.

"Germ of Laziness Found?" *The* [NY] *Sun,* December 5, 1902.

"He has just returned . . .": "Laziness a Disease," *Salt Lake City Herald,* December 9, 1902.

"Dr. Styles is sure . . ." same as above.

"The American scientist . . .": "Due to a Germ," from *Baltimore American,* reprinted in the *Daily Sentinel* [Grand Junction, CO], December 23, 1902.

"It is the privilege . . .": *Albuquerque* [NM] *Daily Citizen,* January 22, 1903.

"There is only one . . .": "Hunting Down the Lazy Germ," *Denver Republican,* quoted in *Washington Post,* October 25, 1903.

"weak in body . . .": "Germ of Laziness," *Goldsboro* [NC] *Weekly Argus*, January 1, 1903.

"It would have taken . . ." and "to direct . . .": Stiles, "Early History," 1939, p. 296.

ALL ABOUT HOOKWORMS (PAGE 42)

"Plain Facts . . .": "The Hookworm: Its Eradication," *Richmond* [VA] *Times-Dispatch*, March 17, 1912.

CHAPTER FIVE
BATTLING *NECATOR* (PAGE 46)

"I believe there are . . .": quoted in "Crusade to Transform the South's 'Poor Whites' into Industrious Citizens," *Washington Post,* September 27, 1908.

"I do not know . . ." and "you will know . . .": quoted by Stiles, June 17, 1908, in North Carolina Board of Health, *Twelfth Biennial Report*, p. 26.

"the inferior mental . . .": Stiles, "Report upon the Prevalence," p. 37.

"In no other disease . . .": H. F. Harris, quoted in Stiles, "Report upon the Prevalence," p. 37.

"not because the country . . .": Stiles, "Report upon the Prevalence," p. 51.

"if he had to choose . . .": quoted in "Summary of Transactions of the Public Health and Marine-Hospital Service, Fiscal Year 1909, and to November 1, 1909," *Public Health Reports,* December 10, 1909, p. 1851.

"that they had never . . ." and "abundant evidence . . .": Stiles, "Report upon the Prevalence," p. 51.

"They were not worth . . .": quoted by Stiles in "Crusade to Transform the South's 'Poor Whites' into Industrious Citizens," *Washington Post,* September 27, 1908.

"The one real hope . . .": Carter, p. 631.

"Is a privy of this kind . . .": RSC, *Fifth Annual Report,* p. 123.

CHAPTER SIX
"SKIDOO HOOKWORM" (PAGE 59)

"Skidoo, Hookworm": "Skidoo, Hookworm," *Washington Post,* October 29, 1909.

"The South is not lazy.": "Hookworm and Pellagra," *Knoxville* [TN] *Sentinel,* quoted in the *Daily Record* [Columbia, SC], November 9, 1909.

"a so-called 'poor white.'": quoted by Stiles in Sullivan, p. 320.

"If he represents . . .": same as above.

"Can that man . . .": quoted in Hendrick, *The Training of an American,* p. 370.

"About fifty cents . . .": same as above, p. 371.

"I have never seen . . .": same as above.

"There are four . . .": same as above.

"below the standard . . .": quoted in "Hurts Tarheel State," *Washington Post,* November 13, 1908.

"a bad tenant . . ." and "broadcast preconceived . . .": Daniels, pp. 567–68.

"The Country Life . . .": *News and Observer,* quoted in Daniels, p. 568.

"had more of the appearance . . ." and "true conditions": Governor Robert Glenn quoted in "Hurts Tarheel State," *Washington Post,* November 13, 1908.

"slandering the land . . .": "Memoranda re: Rockefeller Commission for the Extermination of the Hookworm Disease, October 26, 1909," in Hendrick, *The Training of an American*, p. 373.

"If Doctor Stiles . . .": Dr. Simon Flexnor quoted in Brooks, p. 164.

"offered conclusive . . .": Gates, *Chapters in My Life*, p. 225.

"Perhaps two million . . .": quoted in same as above.

"immediately recognized . . ." and "They saw in its eradication . . .": same as above, p. 226.

"It is the largest . . .": "Memoranda re: Rockefeller Commission for the Extermination of the Hookworm Disease, October 26, 1909, in Hendrick, *The Training of an American,* p. 373.

"This gift is one . . ." and "It means . . .": quoted in "Lazy Bug Joke Dead," *Washington Post,* October 30, 1909.

"aggressive campaign . . .": letter John D. Rockefeller to Rockefeller Sanitary Commission board members, October 26, 1909, in RAC.

"its warm-hearted people" and "their many kindnesses . . .": same as above.

"the states doing . . .": "South Resents Intermeddling, *Birmingham* [AL] *Age-Herald*, November 3, 1909.

"The South is represented . . .": *New Orleans* [LA] *Picayune*, quoted in "Southern Bishop
Hits Rockefeller," *Staunton Spectator* [VA], November 12, 1909.

"but the incident . . .": "Hookworm and Pellagra," *Knoxville* [TN] *Sentinel,* quoted in the
Daily Record [Columbia, SC], November 9, 1909.

"Uncleanliness is not more . . .": G. Grosvenor Dawe quoted in "Hookworm Not Local Evil,"
Washington Post, December 12, 1909.

"There is less hookworm . . .": "Misplaced Benevolence," *Nashville* [TN] *American,* quoted in
Macon [GA] *Daily Telegraph*, November 1, 1909.

"This habit of singling out . . .": letter from Bishop Warren Candler to the *Atlanta* [GA]
Journal, quoted in "Southern Bishop Hits Rockefeller," *Staunton Spectator* [VA],
November 12, 1909.

"Most of the rural schools . . ." and "dangerous agents . . .": quoted in "Gives Cure for
Hookworm," *Washington Post,* November 28, 1909.

CHAPTER SEVEN
HOOKWORM SOCIALS (PAGE 72)

"The scenes at these . . .": letter from F. T. Gates to John D. Rockefeller, April 15, 1912, in RAC.

"The task . . ." and "It will be done . . .": Wickliffe Rose, "Organization, Activities, and
Results up to December 31, 1910," Report of the Administrative Secretary, RSC, *First
Annual Report,* p. 11.

"It looks as though . . .": letter from F. T. Gates to John D. Rockefeller, November 2, 1910,
in RAC.

"One of the fine things . . .": letter from Wickliffe Rose to W. W. Dinsmore, June 17, 1912,
quoted in Ettling, p. 174.

"The results . . ." and "I predict that . . .": letter from Wickliffe Rose to F. T. Gates, June 28,
1911, in RSC, *Second Annual Report*, p. 126.

"Three children . . .": Hookworm Commission, Alabama Board of Health, p. 8.

"Many children have become . . .": "Hookworm Disease in Blount County," *Maryville* [TN]
Times, October 17, 1913.

"a bloodcurdling illustration . . ." and "emaciated boy . . .": Thomas D. Clark, *My Century in
History: Memoirs,* Lexington: University Press of Kentucky, 2006, p. 33.

"It means health . . .": "Hookworm Disease," *Grenada* [MS] *Sentinel*, March 21, 1913.

"We have had a total . . .": letter from Dr. J. S. Lock to Dr. McCormack, May 13, 1913, in
RSC, *Fourth Annual Report,* p. 87.

"certain" and "wonderful.": Columbus County, NC, notice, in RSC, *Second Annual Report,* p. 103.

"the most severe . . .": "Report of the Scientific Secretary," RSC, *Second Annual Report*, p. 131.

CHAPTER EIGHT
THE PRIVY PROBLEM (PAGE 90)

"Thymol in one hand . . .": letter from W. S. Rankin to Wickliffe Rose, January 15, 1912, quoted in Boccaccio, p. 53.

"I do not mean . . .": letter from Stiles to Rose, August 15, 1912, quoted in Ettling, p. 165.

"All fresh human . . ." and "should be accepted . . .": "Report of the Scientific Secretary," RSC, *First Annual Report,* p. 11.

"Probably the pit privy . . .": RSC, *Fifth Annual Report,* p. 26.

"They are cheerful . . .": letter from S. N. Carven to S. H. Jacobs, December 1, 1912, quoted in Ettling, pp. 147–48.

"Human life is . . .": Stiles, "Soil Pollution as Cause of Ground Itch," p. 4.

"You will save . . ." and "just as surely . . .": same as above.

"to make the story . . .": quoted in "Organization, Activities, and Results up to December 31, 1910," Report of the Administrative Secretary RSC, *First Annual Report,* p. 21.

"In short, we have . . .": letter from W. E. Moore, F. R. Corkern, R. W. Magee, and W. R. Seal to Dr. George B. Adams, November 30, 1911, in RSC, *Second Annual Report,* pp. 118–19.

"Surely it is . . ." and "Mothers and fathers . . .": letter from J. A. Harris to the *Telegraph,* in "Dr. Whittle's Work," *Macon* [GA] *Daily Telegraph,* June 17, 1915.

"I wish you . . .": letter from Dr. George F. Lucas, in RSC, *Fourth Annual Report,* p. 101.

"I am now mining . . ." and "and I never feel . . .": letter from Joe McFarland to A. T. McCormack, December 28, 1912, quoted in Boccaccio, p. 43.

"If I had been told . . .": letter from Senator James K. Vardaman to Dr. W. S. Leathers, in RSC, *Fourth Annual Report,* p. 85.

"The [medical] profession. . .": Wickliffe Rose, "Work of the Sanitary Commission," August 13, 1914, p. 5, in RAC.

"so easy to recognize . . ." and "The average Southern . . .": Stiles in "Discussion of 'Tropical Diseases and Public Health,'" *Southern Medical Journal,* Vol. 8 (September 1, 1915), p. 748.

"the most effective . . .": RSC, *Fifth Annual Report,* p. 22.

CHAPTER NINE
A CURSE IS LIFTED (PAGE 103)

"Theoretically, hook-worm . . .": J. B. Elliott, M.D., "The Duty of Our Profession and the Public in the Prevention of Our Most Common Diseases" *Southern Medical Journal,* Vol.4 (November 1911), p. 759.

"Hookworm disease . . .": letter from Frederick T. Gates to John D. Rockefeller, August 19, 1914, quoted in Ettling, p. 198.

"The chief purpose . . .": letter from John D. Rockefeller to the Rockefeller Sanitary Commission for the Eradication of Hookworm Disease, August 12, 1914, in RAC.

"All the peoples . . .": Herbert Quick, "Microscope of Doctor Stiles is Driving Manana from South," *The Day Book* [Chicago, IL], May 13, 1914.

"Hookworm disease . . .": International Health Board, *Thirteenth Annual Report, January 1, 1926–December 31, 1926,* New York: Rockefeller Foundation, 1927, p. 6.

"the public health . . ." Stiles, "Hookworm Disease in Certain Parts of the South: A New Plan of Attack," *Southern Medical Journal,* February 1932, p. 190.

CHAPTER TEN
THE BLOODSUCKER LIVES ON (PAGE 114)

"If the soil were not befouled . . .": Wickliffe Rose, "A Sanitary Survey," *American Journal of Public Health,* Vol. 3 (July 1913), p. 655.

BIBLIOGRAPHY

*Indicates a primary source

*Anderson, Alice L., and Thomas Allen. "Mapping Historic Hookworm Disease Prevalence in the Southern U.S., Comparing Percent Prevalence with Percent Soil Drainage Type Using GIS." *Infectious Diseases: Research and Treatment*, Vol. 4 (2011): 1–9.

*Ashford, Bailey K. "Ankylostomiasis in Puerto Rico." *New York Medical Journal*, Vol. 71 (April 14, 1900): 552–56.

*Ashford, Bailey K., and Pedro Gutierrez Igaravidez. *Uncinariasis (Hookworm Disease) in Porto Rico: A Medical and Economic Problem.* Washington, DC: Government Printing Office, 1911.

*Bartsch, Sarah M., Peter J. Hotez, and others. "The Global Economic and Health Burden of Human Hookworm Infection." *PLOS Neglected Tropical Diseases*, September 8, 2016.

Beardsley, Edward H. *A History of Neglect: Health Care for Blacks and Mill Workers in the Twentieth-Century South.* Knoxville, TN: University of Tennessee Press, 1987.

Bjorkman, Frances Maule. "The Cure for Two Million Sick." *World's Work*, Vol. 48 (May 1909): 11607–12.

*Bleakley, Hoyt. "Disease and Development: Evidence from Hookworm Eradication in the American South." *Quarterly Journal of Economics,* Vol. 122 (2007): 73–117.

Boccaccio, Mary. "Ground Itch and Dew Poison: The Rockefeller Sanitary Commission 1909–14." *Journal of the History of Medicine and Allied Sciences*, Vol. 27 (January 1972): 30–53.

Bogitsh, Burton J., Clint E. Carter, and Thomas N. Oeltmann. *Human Parasitology,* 5th ed. San Diego, CA: Academic Press, 2019.

Brooker, Simon, Jeffrey Bethony, and Peter J. Hotez. "Human Hookworm Infection in the 21st Century." *Advances in Parasitology,* Vol. 58 (2004): 197–288.

Brooks, F. G. "Charles Wardell Stiles, Intrepid Scientist." *Bios.* Vol. 18 (October 1947): 139–69.

Brooks, Frank G. "Charles Wardell Stiles." *Systematic Zoology,* Vol. 13 (December 1964): 220–26.

Brownlow, Louis. "The Passing of the 'Po' White Trash: The Rockefeller Commission's Successful Fight Against the Hookworm Disease." *Hampton-Columbian Magazine,* Vol. 27 (November 1911): 634–46.

Bugnion, E. "On the Epidemic Caused by Ankylostomum Among the Workmen in the St. Gothard Tunnel." *British Medical Journal,* Vol. 1 (March 12, 1881): 382.

Byrd, Hiram. *Hookworm Disease: A Handbook of Information for All Who Are Interested.* St. Augustine, FL: State Board of Health of Florida, October 1910.

Carter, Marion Hamilton. "The Vampire of the South." *McClure's Magazine,* Vol. 33 (October 1909): 617–31.

Cassedy, James H. "'The Germ of Laziness' in the South, 1900–1915: Charles Wardell Stiles and the Progressive Paradox." *Bulletin of the History of Medicine*, Vol. 45 (March–April 1971): 159–69.

*Chapin, Charles V. *A Report on State Public Health Work Based on a Survey of State Boards of Health.* Chicago: American Medical Association, 1916.

Chernow, Ron. *Titan: The Life of John D. Rockefeller, Sr.* New York: Random House, 1998.

*Coelho, Philip R. P., and Robert A. McGuire. "Racial Differences in Disease Susceptibilities: Intestinal Worm Infections in the Early Twentieth-Century American South." *Social History of Medicine*, Vol. 19 (December 2006): 461–82.

*Crompton, D. W. T., and R. R. Whitehead. "Hookworm Infections and Human Iron Metabolism." *Parasitology,* Vol. 107 (Supplement 1993, *Human Nutrition and Parasitic Infection*): S137–45.

Crompton, D. W. T, and Lorenzo Savioli. *Handbook of Helminthiasis for Public Health.* Boca Raton, FL: Taylor & Francis, 2007.

*Daniels, Josephus. *Editor in Politics.* Chapel Hill: University of North Carolina Press, 1941.

Deaderick, William H., and Loyd Thompson. *The Endemic Diseases of the Southern States.* Philadelphia: W. B. Saunders, 1916.

Despommier, Dickson D. *People, Parasites, and Plowshares: Learning from Our Body's Most Terrifying Invaders.* New York: Columbia University Press, 2013.

Despommier, Dickson D., Robert W. Gwadz, Peter J. Hotez, and Charles A. Knirsch. *Parasitic Diseases.* 5th ed. New York: Apple Trees Productions, 2005.

Dock, George A., and Charles C. Bass. *Hookworm Disease: Etiology, Pathology, Diagnosis, Prognosis, Prophylaxis, and Treatment.* St. Louis, MO: C. V. Mosby, 1910.

Duffy, John. *The Sanitarians: A History of American Public Health.* Urbana, IL: University of Illinois Press, 1990.

Elman, Cheryl, Robert A. McGuire, and Barbara Whittman. "Extending Public Health: The Rockefeller Sanitary Commission and Hookworm in the American South." *American Journal of Public Health*, Vol. 104 (January 2014): 47–58.

Ettling, John. *The Germ of Laziness: Rockefeller Philanthropy and Public Health in the New South.* Cambridge, MA: Harvard University Press, 1981.

Farley, John. *To Cast Out Disease: A History of the International Health Division of the Rockefeller Foundation (1913–1951).* New York: Oxford University Press, 2004.

Ferrell, John A. *Hookworm Disease: Its Ravages, Prevention and Cure.* Washington, DC: Rockefeller Sanitary Commission for the Eradication of Hookworm Disease, 1915.

*_____. *The Rural School and Hookworm Disease.* Washington, DC: Government Printing Office, 1914.

*Flowers, Catherine Coleman. *Waste: One Woman's Fight Against America's Dirty Secret.* New York: New Press, 2020.

Furman, Bess. *A Profile of the United States Public Health Service 1798–1948.* Washington, DC: U.S. Department of Health, Education, and Welfare; National Institutes of Health; and National Library of Medicine, 1973.

*Gates, Frederick T. "The Country School of To-Morrow." *World's Work*, Vol. 24 (August 1912): 460–518.

*_____. "The Memoirs of Frederick T. Gates." *American Heritage*, Vol. 6 (April 1955): 71–86.

*Gates, Frederick Taylor. *Chapters in My Life.* New York: Free Press, 1977.

Gilles, H. M., and P. A. J. Ball. *Hookworm Infections.* New York: Elsevier, 1991.

Gillespie, Stephen H., and Richard D. Pearson, eds. *Principles and Practice of Clinical Parasitology.* New York: John Wiley & Sons, 2001.

Hendrick, Burton J. *The Life and Letters of Walter H. Page.* Vol. 1. Garden City, NJ: Doubleday, Page, 1924.

_____. *The Training of an American: The Earlier Life and Letters of Walter H. Page, 1855–1913.* Boston: Houghton Mifflin, 1928.

Holland, Celia V., and Malcolm W. Kennedy. *The Geohelminths: Ascaris, Trichuris and Hookworm.* New York: Kluwer Academic Publishers, 2002.

*Hookworm Commission, Alabama State Board of Health. *Hookworm Disease: A Story of the Hookworm Told in Pictures.* Montgomery, AL: Brown Printing, 1912.

*"Hookworm (Intestinal)." *DPDx—Laboratory Identification of Parasites of Public Health Concern, Centers for Disease Control and Prevention.* cdc.gov/dpdx/hookworm. Accessed September 1, 2021.

*Hotez, Peter J., Jeff Bethony, and others. "Hookworm: 'The Great Infection of Mankind.'" *PLOS Medicine,* Vol. 2 (March 2005): 0187–91.

Humphreys, Margaret. "How Four Once Common Diseases Were Eliminated from the American South." *Health Affairs,* Vol. 28 (November/December 2009): 1734–44.

John, David T., and William A. Petri, Jr. *Markell and Voge's Medical Parasitology.* 9th ed. St. Louis, MO: Saunders Elsevier, 2006.

*Kean, B. H., Kenneth E. Mott, and Adair J. Russell. *Tropical Medicine and Parasitology: Classic Investigations,* Vol. 2. Ithaca, NY: Cornell University Press, 1978.

*Keller, Alvin E., W. S. Leathers, and Paul M. Densen. "The Results of Recent Studies of Hookworm in Eight Southern States." *American Journal of Tropical Medicine,* Vol. 20 (July 1940): 493–509.

Leavitt, Judith Walzer, and Ronald L. Numbers, eds. *Sickness and Health in America: Readings in the History of Medicine and Public Health.* 3rd ed. Madison, WI: University of Wisconsin Press, 1997.

*Looss, A. *The Anatomy and Life History of Agchylostoma Duodenale Dub.: A Monograph.* Translated by Matilda Bernard. Cairo: National Printing Department, 1905.

Lowry, Thomas Power. *The Yankees' Secret Weapon: Even Lincoln Didn't Know.* Portland, OR: Idle Winter Press, 2016.

*Lumsden, L. L, Norman Roberts, and Ch. Wardell Stiles, "Preliminary Note on a Simple and Inexpensive Apparatus for Use in Safe Disposal of Night Soil." *Public Health Reports,* Vol. 25 (November 11, 1910): 1621–23.

Lynn, Mary K., Josephine A. Morrissey, and Donaldson F. Conserve. "Soil-Transmitted Helminths in the USA: A Review of Five Common Parasites and Future Directions for Avenues of Enhanced Epidemiologic Inquiry." *Current Tropical Medicine Reports,* Vol. 8 (January 30, 2021): 32–42.

Martin, Mike G., and Margaret E. Humphreys. "Social Consequences of Disease in the American South, 1900–World War II." *Southern Medical Journal,* Vol. 99 (August 2006): 862–64.

*McKenna, Megan L., Shannon McAtee, and others. "Human Intestinal Parasite Burden and Poor Sanitation in Rural Alabama." *American Journal of Tropical Medicine and Hygiene,* Vol. 97 (November 8, 2017): 1623–28.

Mullan, Fitzhugh. *Plagues and Politics: The Story of the United States Public Health Service.* New York: Basic Books, 1989.

*North Carolina Board of Health. *Bulletin.* Vol. 27 (April 1912–March 1913).

*North Carolina Board of Health. *Twelfth Biennial Report of the North Carolina Board of Health, 1907–1908.* Raleigh: E. M. Uzzell, 1909.

Nuwer, Rachel. "How a Worm Gave the South a Bad Name." *Nova,* PBS, April 27, 2016. pbs.org/wgbh/nova/article/how-a-worm-gave-the-south-a-bad-name. Accessed September 1, 2021.

Palmer, Steven. "Migrant Clinics and Hookworm Science: Peripheral Origins of International Health, 1840–1920." *Bulletin of the History of Medicine,* Vol. 83 (Winter 2009): 676–709.

Peduzzi, R., and J. C. Piffaretti. "Ancylostoma duodenale and the Saint Gothard Anaemia." *British Medical Journal,* Vol. 287 (December 1983): 1942–45.

*Rockefeller Archive Center. *Rockefeller Foundation: A Digital History.* rockfound.rockarch.org. Accessed September 1, 2021.

*Rockefeller Foundation International Health Commission. *Report on Work for the Relief and Control of Uncinariasis in Southern United States From Jan. 1, 1910, to June 30, 1915.* New York: Rockefeller Foundation, 1915.

*Rockefeller Sanitary Commission for the Eradication of Hookworm Disease. *Annual Reports (First through Fifth) for the Years 1910, 1911, 1912, 1913, 1914.* Washington, DC: Office of the Commission, 1910, 1911, 1912, 1913, 1914, 1915.

Savitt, Todd L., and James Harvey Young, eds. *Disease and Distinctiveness in the American South.* Knoxville, TN: University of Tennessee Press, 1988.

Schwartz, Benjamin. "A Brief Resume of Dr. Stiles' Contributions to Parasitology." *Journal of Parasitology,* Vol. 19 (June 1933): 257–61.

Shubinski, Barbara. "Public Health: How the Fight Against Hookworm Helped Build a System."*RE:source, Rockefeller Archive Center,* April 23, 2020. resource.rockarch.org/story/public-health-how-the-fight-against-hookworm-helped-build-a-system. Accessed September 1, 2021.

Sledge, Daniel. *Health Divided: Public Health and Individual Medicine in the Making of the Modern American State.* Lawrence, KS: University Press of Kansas, 2017.

Sledge, Daniel David. "Southern Maladies: Politics and Public Health in the Pre–Civil Rights South, 1902–1950." PhD diss., Cornell University, 2010.

*"Soil-Transmitted Helminth Infections." *World Health Organization,* March 2, 2020. who.int/news-room/fact-sheets/detail/soil-transmitted-helminth-infections.

State of the World's Sanitation: An Urgent Call to Transform Sanitation for Better Health, Environments, Economies and Societies. New York: United Nations Children's Fund and the World Health Organization, 2020.

*Stiles, Charles Wardell. "Decrease of Hookworm Disease in the United States," *Public Health Reports,* Vol. 45 (August 1, 1930): 1763–81.

*_____."Early History, in Part Esoteric, of the Hookworm (Uncinariasis) Campaign in our Southern United States." *Journal of Parasitology,* Vol. 25 (August 1939): 283–308.

*_____. "Hookworm Disease in Certain Parts of the South: A New Plan of Attack." *Southern Medical Journal,* Vol. 25 (February 1932): 189–92.

*_____. *Hookworm Disease (or Ground-Itch Anemia): Its Nature, Treatment and Prevention.* Public Health Bulletin No. 32, Treasury Department, Public Health and Marine-Hospital Service of the United States. Washington, DC: Government Printing Office, 1910.

*_____. "Hookworm Disease in Its Relation to the Negro." *Public Health Reports*, Vol. 24 (July 30, 1909): 1083–89.

*_____. "Hook-worm Disease in the South—Frequency of Infection by the Parasite (*Uncinaria americana)* in Rural Districts." *Public Health Reports,* Vol. 17 (October 24, 1902): 2433–44.

*_____. "Hookworm Disease in Three Cotton Mills in North Carolina." *Public Health Reports,* Vol. 25 (March 25, 1910): 354–55.

*_____. "Is It Fair to Say That Hookworm Disease Has Almost Disappeared from the United States?" *Science,* Vol. 77 (March 3, 1933): 237–39.

*_____."A New Species of Hookworm *(Uncinaria americana)* Parasitic in Man." *American Medicine,* Vol. 3 (May 10, 1902): 777–78.

*_____. *Report on Condition of Woman and Child Wage-Earners in the United States in 19 Volumes, Vol. 17: Hookworm Disease Among Cotton-Mill Operatives.* Washington: Government Printing Office, 1912.

*_____. *Report upon the Prevalence and Geographic Distribution of Hookworm Disease (Uncinariasis or Anchylostomiasis) in the United States,* Hygienic Laboratory—Bulletin No. 10. Washington, DC: Government Printing Office: February 1903.

*_____. "The Sanitary Privy." *Public Health Reports,* Vol. 25 (April 29, 1910): 545–52.

*_____. *The Sanitary Privy: Its Purpose and Construction.* Public Health Bulletin No. 37, Treasury Department, Public Health and Marine-Hospital Service of the United States. Washington: Government Printing Office, 1919.

*_____. *Soil Pollution as Cause of Ground-Itch, Hookworm Disease (Ground-Itch Anemia), and Dirt Eating.* Washington, DC: Rockefeller Sanitary Commission for the Eradication of Hookworm Disease, 1910.

*_____. "The Surface Privy as a Factor in Soil Pollution, with Resulting Hookworm Disease and Typhoid Fever." *Public Health Reports,* Vol. 24 (October 1, 1909): 1445–47.

*_____. The Treatment of Hookworm Disease." *Public Health Reports,* Vol. 24 (August 20, 1909): 1191–93.

*Strosnider, C. F. "Hookworm Disease, Prevalence, Harmful Results and Treatment." *Journal of the American Medical Association,* Vol. 56 (April 8, 1911): 1024–27.

Sullivan, Mark. *Our Times: The United States, 1900–1925,* Vol. 3, *Pre-War America.* New York: Charles Scribner's Sons, 1930, pp. 312–32.

Troesken, Werner. *Water, Race, and Disease.* Cambridge, MA: MIT Press, 2004.

Williams, Greer. *The Plague Killers.* New York: Charles Scribner's Sons, 1969.

Young, James Harvey. *The Toadstool Millionaires: A Social History of Patent Medicines in America before Federal Regulation.* Princeton, NJ: Princeton University Press, 1961.

ADDITIONAL ARTICLES FROM THESE SOURCES:

American Journal of Nursing
American Journal of Public Health
American Journal of Sociology
American Journal of Tropical Medicine and Hygiene
*Annual Report of the Supervising Surgeon General of the Public Health
  and Marine-Hospital Service of the United States*
Birmingham [AL] *Age-Herald*
British Medical Journal
Chicago Daily Tribune
Human Biology
International Journal for Parasitology
Journal of the American Medical Association
Journal of Bioeconomics
Lancet
Macon [GA] *Daily Telegraph*
Nashville [TN] *American*
New York Sun
New York Times
Public Health Reports
Richmond [VA] *Times-Dispatch*
Social Sciences and Humanities Open
Southern Medical Journal
Staunton [VA] *Spectator*
Trends in Parasitology
Vaccine
Virulence
Washington Post

INDEX

Page numbers in **boldface** refer to images and/or captions

PICTURE CREDITS

Bailey K. Ashford and Pedro Gutierrez Igaravidez. *Uncinariasis (Hookworm Disease) in Porto Rico: A Medical and Economic Problem.* Washington, DC: Government Printing Office, 1911: 26.

Hiram Byrd. *Hookworm Disease: A Handbook of Information for All Who Are Interested.* St. Augustine, FL: State Board of Health of Florida, October 1910: 37, 39.

Centers for Disease Control and Prevention: Global Health, Division of Parasitic Diseases and Malaria: 43 (top), 44, 117 (bottom), 120 (top and bottom); Public Health Image Library: 42 (left), 43 (bottom), 45 (left); by Dr. Mae Melvin: 43 (middle); by James Gathany: 121; by Alaine Kathryn Knipes, Parasitic Disease Branch, Division of Parasitic Diseases and Malaria: 123.

Denver Republican, reprinted in *Washington* [DC] *Post*, October 25, 1903: 41 (top right).

George A. Dock and Charles C. Bass. *Hookworm Disease: Etiology, Pathology, Diagnosis, Prognosis, Prophylaxis, and Treatment.* St. Louis, MO: C. V. Mosby, 1910: 45 (right), 48.

Flickr: "Gotthard Train Tunnel from 1882" by Kecko: 19; by U. S. Army Southern European Task Force, Africa: 118; by USAID: 122.

H. F. Harris. *Pellagra*, NY: Macmillan, 1919: 58.

Hookworm Commission, Alabama State Board of Health. *Hookworm Disease: A Story of the Hookworm Told in Pictures.* Montgomery, AL: Brown Printing, 1912: 33, 88 (top left and right).

Library of Congress, Prints & Photographs Division, LC-DIG-ppmsca-09485: 49. African American Photographs Assembled for 1900 Paris Exposition Collection: LC-USZ62-103813: 38 (top). Bain Collection: LC-B2-3270-13: 60. C. M. Bell Studio Collection: LC-B5-51026B: 27. National Child Labor Committee Collection: LC-DIG-nclc-00414: 38 (bottom); LC-DIG-nclc-01426: 53 (top); LC-DIG-nclc-02932: 53 (bottom); LC-DIG-nclc-04355: 110 (top); LC-DIG-nclc-04354: 110 (bottom); LC-DIG-nclc-04357: 111. National Photo Company Collection: LC-F82-249: 28. U.S. Farm Security Administration/Office of War Information Black-and-White Negatives: LC-USF34-051377-D: 107; LC-USF34-019981-E: 112 (top left); LC-USF34-017376-C: 112 (top right); LC-USF34-009325-C: 112 (bottom); LC-USF34-032903-D: 113; LC-USF34-080026-E: 115.

London Illustrated Times, May 20, 1882: 18.

A. Looss. *The Anatomy and Life History of Agchylostoma Duodenale Dub.: A Monograph.* Translated by Matilda Bernard. Cairo: National Printing Department, 1905: 16.

L. L. Lumsden, Norman Roberts, and Ch. Wardell Stiles. "Preliminary Note on a Simple and Inexpensive Apparatus for Use in Safe Disposal of Night Soil." *Public Health Reports*, Vol. 25 (November 11, 1910): 92.

Macon [GA] *Daily Telegraph,* November 3, 1909: 67.

S. H. McLean, Secretary. *Report of the Board of Health of Mississippi from September 30, 1909 to June 30, 1911.* Nashville, TN: Brandon Printing, 1911: 46.

National Library of Medicine: 22-23, 25, 91 (bottom), 105 (bottom).

New York Sun, December 5, 1902: 40.

North Carolina Digital Collections, Health Services Laboratory Section, Health Services Records, State Archives of North Carolina: 82 (bottom).

Pixabay, by Swadhin Das: 119 (top); by Se Kimseng: 119 (bottom).

Puck, February 27, 1901: 71 (left); May 3, 1905: 71 (right).

Courtesy of the **Rockefeller Archive Center,** Rockefeller Foundation records, photographs: 42 (right), 69, 74 (top), 76, 82 (top), 83, 94 (bottom), 105 (top), 106, 108, 109, 126–127; Rockefeller Family photographs: 70.

Rockefeller Sanitary Commission for the Eradication of Hookworm Disease. *Annual Reports.* Washington, DC: Office of the Commission, 1911–1915. *Fifth Annual Report for the Year 1914:* 8, 94 (top), 97, 99 (top and bottom), 100; *Fourth Annual Report for the Year 1913:* 36, 61, 75, 80 (bottom), 84, 87 (left), 87 (right top and bottom), 93, 98 ; *Third Annual Report for the Year 1912:* 74 (bottom), 80 (top), 88 (bottom left and right), 89 (left and right), 91 (top), 130; *Second Annual Report for the Year 1911:* 85, 86 (left and right).

Courtesy of **David Scharf/Science Source,** cover, 15, 32, 135.

Semi-Weekly Journal [Atlanta], December 8, 1902: 41 (left) .

Sequachee Valley [TN] *News,* August 8, 1912: 81.

Charles Wardell Stiles. *Hookworm Disease (or Ground-Itch Anemia): Its Nature Treatment and Prevention.* Public Health Bulletin No. 32, Treasury Department, Public Health and Marine-Hospital Service of the United States. Washington, DC: Government Printing Office, 1910: 50 (top and bottom).

USDA National Agricultural Library, Special Collections: 13, 35.

Washington Post, October 29, 1909: 66.

Wellcome Collection, Adrian Wressel, Heart of England NHS FT: 117 (top).

The World [New York], December 8, 1902: 41 (bottom right).

World's Work, August 1912: 62.

GAIL JARROW'S SELECT CALKINS CREEK TITLES

MEDICAL FIASCOES SERIES

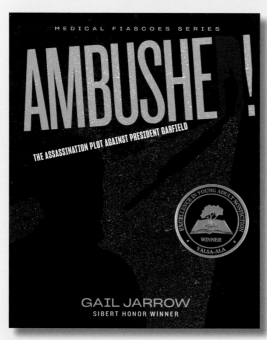

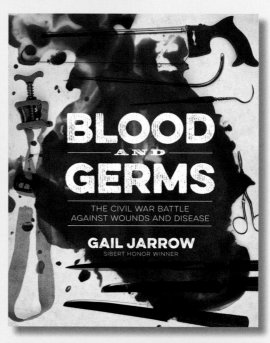

Ambushed! The Assassination Plot Against President Garfield

Winner of the YALSA Award for Excellence in Nonfiction for Young Adults

Kirkus Reviews Best Book
(Middle-Grade History)

CCBC Choice—
Cooperative Children's Book Center

Booklist, Kirkus Reviews, School Library Journal, starred reviews

Blood and Germs: The Civil War Battle Against Wounds and Disease

Kirkus Reviews Best Book
(Middle-Grade Nonfiction)

Outstanding Science Trade Book for Students K–12—
National Science Teaching Association and Children's Book Council

CCBC Choice—
Cooperative Children's Book Center

Orbis Pictus Recommended Book—
National Council of Teachers of English

Best Informational Book for Older Readers—
Chicago Public Library

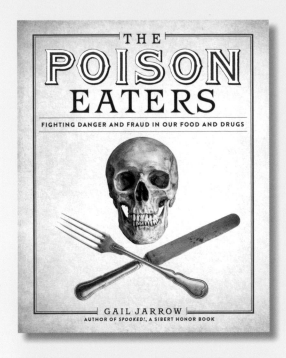

The Poison Eaters:
Fighting Danger and Fraud in Our Food and Drugs

Orbis Pictus Award for Outstanding Nonfiction for Children Honor Book—
National Council of Teachers of English

Notable Children's Book—
Association for Library Service to Children (ALSC/ALA)

Outstanding Science Trade Book for Students—
National Science Teaching Association and Children's Book Council

Notable Social Studies Trade Book for Young People—
National Council for the Social Studies and Children's Book Council

Best Children's Book—Bank Street College of Education

Kirkus Reviews Best Book (Middle-Grade History)

Blue Ribbons List—Bulletin of the Center for Children's Books

Editors' Choice: Books for Youth—Booklist

Lasting Connections, Top 30—Book Links

Best Children's Book—Washington Post

Spooked!: How a Radio Broadcast and *The War of the Worlds* Sparked the 1938 Invasion of America

Robert F. Sibert Award Honor Book—
Association for Library Service to Children/
American Library Association

Golden Kite Honor, Nonfiction for Older Readers—
Society of Children's Book Writers and Illustrators

Notable Children's Book—
Association for Library Service to Children (ALSC/ALA)

Notable Social Studies Trade Book for Young Readers—
National Council for the Social Studies and Children's Book Council

Excellence in Nonfiction Award Nominee—
Young Adult Library Services Association

Quick Picks for Reluctant Young Adult Readers—
Young Adult Library Services Association

Editors' Choice List—Booklist

Best Book—School Library Journal

Blue Ribbons List for Nonfiction—
Bulletin of the Center for Children's Books

CCBC Choices Best of the Year—Cooperative Children's Book Center

Best Children's Book of the Year—Bank Street College of Education

Best Children's Book—Washington Post

DEADLY DISEASES TRILOGY

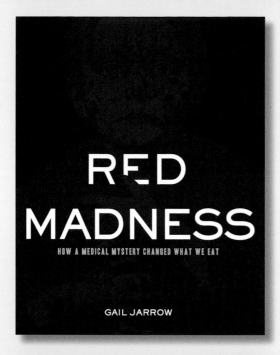

Red Madness: How a Medical Mystery Changed What We Eat

Jefferson Cup for Older Readers—
Virginia Library Association

Best Book—
School Library Journal

Best STEM Book—
National Science Teaching Association
and the Children's Book Council

Best Children's Book of the Year, Science—
Bank Street College of Education

CCBC Choice—
Copperative Children's Book Center

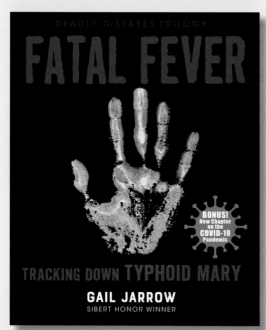

Fatal Fever: Tracking Down Typhoid Mary

Eureka! Gold Award—
California Reading Association

Blue Ribbons List for Nonfiction—
Bulletin of the Center for Children's Books

CCBC Choice—
Cooperative Children's Book Center

Best Children's Book of the Year, Outstanding Merit—
Bank Street College of Education

Nonfiction Honor List—VOYA

Bubonic Panic: When Plague Invaded America

Best Book—
School Library Journal

Best Book for Teens/Best Teen Mysteries and Thrillers—
Kirkus Reviews

Eureka! Gold Award—
California Reading Association

Outstanding Science Trade Book for Students—
National Science Teaching Association
and the Children's Book Council

Recommended, National Science Teaching Association

Notable Social Studies Trade Book—
National Council for the Social Studies and Children's Book Council

CCBC Choice—
Cooperative Children's Book Center

Best Books for Teens—
New York Public Library

GAIL JARROW is the author of books about medical mysteries, deadly diseases, and other intriguing stories from the history of science. Her latest series, Medical Fiascoes, includes *Blood and Germs*, *Ambushed!*, and *American Murderer*. Gail's work has received many distinctions, including the YALSA Award for Excellence in Nonfiction for Young Adults; the Sibert Honor Book medal; an NSTA Best STEM Book and Outstanding Science Trade Book; an ILA Best Science Book; Orbis Pictus Honor and Recommended Books; and the Children's Book Guild Nonfiction Award. Gail has a degree in zoology and has taught science to young students of all ages. She lives in Ithaca, New York. Visit gailjarrow.com.